S0-AXI-849

Negritude Agonistes, Assimilation against Nationalism in the French-speaking Caribbean and Guyane

Negritude Agonistes, Assimilation against Nationalism in the French-speaking Caribbean and Guyane

Christian Filostrat

Africana Homestead Legacy Publishers
Cherry Hill, New Jersey

Africana Homestead Legacy Publishers
100 Springdale Road Ste A3 # 206
Cherry Hill, New Jersey 08003 USA
e-mail: editors@ahlpub.com or book-orders@ahlpub.com

Some material in this book was reprinted from published works by Christian Filostrat: "La Négritude et la 'Conscience raciale et révolution sociale' d'Aimé Césaire," *Presence Francophone*, Vol. 21, 1980, and "Cesaire's Negritude: Clarion call to independence," *The Western Journal of Black Studies,* Vol. 5(1), Spring 1981. The author thanks the publishers of each journal for the permission to reprint.

Photographs and other illustrations are from the collection of the author.

Printed and bound in the United States of America.
11 10 09 08 5 4 3 2 1

This paper meets the requirements of ANSI/NISO Z39.48-1992 (R 1997) Permanence of Paper.

Library of Congress Cataloging-in-Publication Data

Filostrat, Christian.
Negritude agonistes, assimilation against nationalism in the French-speaking Caribbean and Guyane / Christian Filostrat.
p. cm.
Includes bibliographical references and index.
Summary: "Assesses European and French colonialism in the Caribbean from the 16th century and the racial and cultural movements of black and mixed-race people in the French-speaking West Indies and Guyane that emerged in the 19th century and first half of the 20th century"--Provided by publisher.
ISBN 978-0-9818939-2-1 (hardcover : alk. paper)
1. West Indies, French--History. 2. French Guiana--History. 3. France--Colonies--History--West Indies, French. 4. Blacks--Race identity--West Indies, French--History. 5. Blacks--Cultural assimilation--West Indies, French--History. 6. Blacks--Race identity--French Guiana--History. 7. Blacks--Cultural assimilation--French Guiana--History. I. Title.

F2151.F55 2008
972.97'600496--dc22

2008045871

In memory of these friends and negritude proponents, Marietta Campos Damas da Bahia, Wilfred Cartey, Robert J. Cummings.

Contents

Preface

The issue of racial consciousness and cultural identity among people of African descent in the Caribbean has been the subject of many studies. Writing in 1960, V.S. Naipaul argued that, largely because he lived in a borrowed culture, more than other people, the West Indian needed writers to tell him who he was and where he stood in the world.[1]

In the case of the French-speaking Caribbean and Guyane (French-ruled Guiana), writers of the Haitianist and Negritude Schools made pronounced attempts in this direction in the 1930s and 1940s. This exposé identifies why they failed to make any measurable change in the sociopolitical existence of their countries.

This is first an account of the consequence of France's colonization of the Caribbean and Guyane through a general overview of the history and analysis of the relation of forces and peoples in Haiti, Guyane, Guadeloupe, and Martinique. Next, Haiti's literary elite take center stage to elucidate through their poetry the effect Haiti's history has had on them and vice versa as well as the resultant sociopolitical condition befalling their country. Along the line of using poets to illuminate these colonial societies' perspectives and to bring into sharper focus the history of the French-speaking West Indies, writers from Martinique, Guyane, and Guadeloupe reveal why there is a continuing French presence in the Caribbean.

This study is also an effort to come to grips with the differences between Haitianism and Negritude as it considers the historical, socio-political, and literary roots and dimensions from which both arose.

The profit motive led the European powers into a race for the "New World," culminating, ultimately, in wars and territorial compartmentalization. Later, the production of sugar required a greater supply of workers than had tobacco farming. In Africa, the Europeans found the supply whose extraction — in the words of Walter Rodney — would also underdevelop the black continent.[2] The "discovery" of the Indies and the beginning of primitive capital formation in Europe led to the uprooting of millions of blacks from Africa and thousands of white indentured servants from Europe. In time, there arose a master-slave society and a pot-pourri of African and European cultures, dominated by western values derived from the Catholic ideal in St. Domingue, Guadeloupe, Guyane, and Martinique, France's "place in the sun."

In order to maintain their domination over this new society and overcome their numerical weakness, by the middle of the 19th century, the French had imposed in their Caribbean colonies their peculiar system of amalgamation. Unlike the British who considered their imperial territories as peripheral to the British Isles, the French made their overseas territories integral parts of France. To reach this goal, the French called for a policy of integration and assimilation of the inhabitants and territories of the French-speaking West Indies and Guyane, notably following St. Domingue's revolution.

Important consequences accompanied the implementation of this policy, designed to create a subservient class to uphold France's colonial dominance. It created, for example, a dual community within the society of the colonized. On the one hand, there were the French-trained elite of color that became an integral part of the colonial enterprise. As this elite sought to strike an economic and intellectual alliance with France, it chose France's ways of life and socialized itself into accepting the tenet that to prevail one had to acquire French colonial values. Concomitantly, this class upheld the western view that Africa was a heathen abode with no culture or worthwhile civilization. As Jack Moddis says, colonialism succeeded in perpetuating itself in Africa, Asia, Latin America and the West Indies, because not only it had the means of violence at its disposal but also, most importantly, because it managed to win important native groups to its side.[3] On the other hand, there were the blacks. Outsiders to the colonial bourgeois society, they were the reactive agents of colonialism, conditioned into assuming that in order to throw off the shackles of slavery one had to repudiate Africa. Africa had become synonymous with slavery and slavery with African blackness and negroness.

To prevent rebellions and revolts, the small colony of whites, encouraged by the metropolitan policymakers, embarked upon a system of ethnic balkanization. However, St. Domingue, due mainly to its greater need for slaves, escaped from this policy. The result was the slave revolt, which created the independent nation of Haiti in 1804.

Moreover, although the mother country implemented a policy of linguistic imperialism, there nevertheless developed, due to ethnic amalgamation, an admixture of African and European languages resulting in a Creole language typical of the French speaking West Indies.

This study seeks to assess four aspects of the French colonial enterprise in the Caribbean. First, it examines the black and the people of color's desire for cultural and socio-political assimilation into France, and appraises the expansion of the black educated elite and its relationship to France concerning the status of the colonies.

Second, it shows that the racial and cultural consciousness that took place in Haiti during and following its 1915–1934 United States occupation was an indigenous movement whose purpose was the rehabilitation of Haiti's culture for the benefit of the Haitian elite. Haitianism, therefore, is not part of the student movement in Paris between the two World Wars whose goal was to denounce the system of French assimilation and the status of the colonies at the time.

Third, it compares and contrasts the movement of Haitianism with Negritude concerning Africa. It argues that, whereas the Haitians could draw from the well of their own Afro-Haitian culture to reach Africa, the Negritude proponents considered themselves exiles from Africa — moreover alienated from any original West Indian or Guyanese culture.

Fourth, it demonstrates that socio-political conditions in France played a pivotal role in the movement that led to the rise of the school of Negritude. As a concomitant of its colonial policies, the French government created an educational system that required students to go to France for their university degrees and, sometimes, high school diplomas. In 1932 the mother country became the cradle of the movement to counter the French policy of assimilation, when a group of university students from the French-speaking West Indies and Guyane proposed a *New French Negro* guiding principle to overhaul their colonial society.

One of the questions discussed is, what motivated the students of 1932 to start denouncing the colonial status-quo of their society? These students could have, following the example of their elders, joined the colonial administrative machinery and lived comfortably, at the end of their studies in France.

This study covers the period ranging from the beginning of European interest in the Caribbean to 1946; involving discussion of the foundation of the French West Indies, slavery, emancipation, and colonization. The years 1928 and 1932 are respectively Haitianism and Negritude starting dates. They stand as frames of reference for, in the case of Haitianism, Jean Price-Mars's denunciation of the American occupation of Haiti; and in the case of Negritude, a group of students' assault against assimilation.

1946 is the year the French-speaking West Indies and Guyane became *départements* (counties) of France. That same year, the Estimé revolution took place in Haiti in the name of Haitianism.

The study concludes with a discussion of the culturo-political paradox of Negritude in the Caribbean and Guyane through a discussion of the Aimé Césaire principle which opposes political self-determination at least for Martinique where Césaire held total sway for over fifty years — against the background of an interview with Frantz Fanon's widow, Josie Fanon, part of which addresses the issue of national liberation.

Introduction
Spain's Gambit

In his effort to find a new passage to the Orient, Christopher Columbus set foot in the Caribbean in 1492 and claimed the erroneously named "Indies" for Spain. One year later, the Treaty of Tordesillas and the issuance of the Pontifical Bulls bestowed official blessings upon the venture.

Columbus, (whose name in Spanish—Cristobal Colon—stands for Christbearer and Colonizer), erected crucifixes at each new place of discovery and inquired about gold at every port—bullion being of primary importance to the economy of colonial Spain's budding mercantilist economy.

The shipments of precious metals, which regularly crossed the treacherous Atlantic waters on the way to Spain, brought to the area scores of Dutch, Danish, French, British privateers and pirates in search of quick riches. Their light brigantines would out sail and pounce upon the heavily laden Spanish galleons. Much to the chagrin of the kings of Spain, his ships were quickly unloaded and relieved of their prized cargo before resting at the bottom of the sea.

The men and women who searched the seas for the Spain-bound precious metals were among the first Europeans to settle in the Caribbean isles. That they were outlaws in their own countries gave the other European powers a diplomatic way out to challenge Spain's hegemony in the West Indies. In the case of France, the privateers also controlled the settlements, which later would constitute the colonies of Martinique, Guadeloupe, St. Domingue, and Guyane.

Prodded by his royal sponsors, Columbus during this third voyage began to emphasize the need for colonization and land cultivation rather than the search solely for gold. He also received the right to take convicts to populate Hispaniola (St. Domingue).

As an admiral, Columbus may have had no equal in his day; but, as the Americas' first Spanish viceroy, he was a failure. His harsh rule compounded by nepotism (he made his brothers Giacomo and Bartolome mayor and governor of Isabella and Santo Tomas, respectively) drove the settlers to rebellion. Thus, when Columbus returned on his third expedition, he found that the new mayor of Isabella, Francisco Roldan, had rebelled openly against his rule. The compromise that resulted between the two men unleashed the system of encomienda on the Caribbean. This system, formalized by the crown and placed under the administration of Nicolas Ovando, provided each colonist with free labor as well as tribute in gold dust from Hispaniola's natives. In return, each colonist was to provide protection for "his" natives and contribute to the maintenance of the parish priest. The encomienda system, instituted the year following Columbus's arrival in the Caribbean, laid waste to the Indian population of Hispaniola.

The destruction of the island's native population through slavery, physical and mental abuse that eroded the natives' desire to survive coupled with lack of immunity to European diseases created a labor shortage in Hispaniola. The immediate replacements for the Caribs were not from Africa but from Europe. They ran the gamut of European society, ranging from hospital patients, landless aristocrats, convicts, and indigents. However, all were Catholic.

Voluntarily or otherwise, this cadre of ill-assorted, mismatched settlers, all took a common ship that led them to new adventures in the "Indies." The proclamation from the king and queen of Spain, issued in 1497, is illustrative of the means employed to secure citizens for Hispaniola:

> ... we have commanded the loading of certain ships and vessels in which there will go certain people who have been paid for a certain time, and because they are not enough for the development of a town as befits the service of God and ours, if other people do not go to reside and live and serve in them at their own cost, we wishing to provide for this, issue this our decree...that each and every male person who may have committed ... any murders or any other crimes of what ever nature and quality they might be, except heresy and lese majeste...shall go and serve in person in Hispaniola, at their own cost, as commanded by the Admiral in our name. Those who deserve a minor penalty than death ... for a year and will be pardoned.[1]

This decree validates the notion that, besides Dominican friars and later Jesuit priests, few persons of means and education settled in the early Spanish colony.

The Spanish government had given Castile preferential treatment in matters of colonial trade and population. Castile, however, could not meet the labor needs of Hispaniola. The government had to relax its ban against non-Catholics and began the wholesale emigration of Spaniards. In 1518 the Spanish authorities offered free passage, free plots of land, and free livestock to anyone who would emigrate; but, in spite of such inducements, the shortage of colonists continued. In fact, the situation worsened when tales of gold discoveries in Peru and New Spain reached

Hispaniola where the precious metal had petered out. Europeans were never able to fill the labor trough emptied by the destruction of the Caribs.

The annihilation of the Caribs, as is often told, came to the attention of the priest-encomendero, Bartolome de las Casas, who, to protect against their complete decimation, proposed that Africans be brought to Hispaniola as replacements. Seemingly, the wholesale introduction of Africans to the Indies was triggered by the fact that by the time Columbus made his discoveries in the Caribbean, the Portuguese using slave laborers had already begun the successful cultivation and harvesting of sugar cane in Sao Tomé, an island off the west coast of Africa.

Europeans of this and subsequent eras believed that Africans could endure the arduous and often killing toil that neither the Caribs nor their own societal dregs could withstand. In a letter dated January 22, 1518, Alonzo Zuaro, judge of Hispaniola, wrote to Cardinal Ximenes, regent of Spain, "indeed, there is urgent need for Negro slaves. The burden of work of the Indians will be eased and unlimited ... gold will be mined. This is the best land in the world for Negroes, women and old men, and it is very rarely that one of these people die."[2]

By the middle of the sixteenth century, the cry from Hispaniola for more African slaves reached a crescendo. The king was still concerned, however, about introducing non-Catholics to the island, and limited the captive Africans sent to Hispaniola to those living in Spain. In 1501 he wrote to the governor of Hispaniola that because:

our earnest desire for ... conversion ... might be impeded, we cannot consent to the immigration of Moors, heretics, Jews, re-converts, or persons newly converted to our Holy faith unless they are Negro or other slaves who have been in the power of Christians who are our subjects and nationals and carry our express permission.[3]

The requests for more Africans ran unabated, nonetheless. To be sure, religion was no match for economic considerations. Spain did not have enough "Negro or other slaves born in the power of Christians" to fill all the requests. Not only was there a severe shortage of Christianized enslaved Africans, but equally vital, the Africans themselves began to refute the myth that they could toil ad infinitum without succumbing. Ferdinand mused, "I do not understand why so many Negroes have died."[4] The basic difference between the slave labor of the Caribs and that of the Africans is understandable. Whereas the Carib population was limited in number, to the European slavers, the Africans seemed a resource without limit.

In 1455 Pope Nicholas V gave the Portuguese the key to the captive African chest:

> We, after scrupulous reflection, are granting by our Bull, full and entire freedom to King Alphonso to conquer, to besiege, to fight, and to submit all the Saracens, Pagans, and other enemies of Christ, wherever they may be; and to seize the kingdoms, the dukedoms, the princedoms, the lordships, personal properties, landed properties, and all the wealth they withhold and possess; and to submit these people to perpetual slavery; to transmit them to their successors; to take advantage and make use of them personally and with their offspring[5]

The Church of Rome stood as the final arbiter and the ultimate legalizer in another age when money, power, armadas, and strong alliances ruled the economic order. The Church had not circumvented the teaching of Him in whose name it preached. Rather, it had distorted the words of Christ in order to rationalize the activities of the two bastions of Christendom, Portugal and Spain. By the fifteenth century, the Church, after hundreds of years of abuse and Roman politics, faced rising Protestantism—first from Germany, then England and finally the Low Countries. The Great Schism (1309–1420) compounded by the Babylonian Captivity of the Avignon Popes, which lasted until the advent of Pope Nicholas V, had left the papacy in chaos and in dire need of support. For such support the Pope paid, in part, with pronouncements such as the aforementioned Bull. This Bull, which put Christendom's stamp of approval on the wholesale enslavement of Africans, was a monopolistic device favoring King Alphonso of Portugal.

Nicholas V was called "the great humanist" for his erudition as well as for his contributions to the Vatican library. He, however, typified the ecclesiastical ruler of an age whose worldly concerns overrode spiritual leadership. The Pope's grant to the King of Portugal carried no more weight than did the Pope himself. Simultaneously, having found what they believed to be the answer to the labor shortage in the Caribbean, North America, and Latin America, the other European powers quickly defied the Pope and Portugal's patent on the African slave trade.

Entire libraries exist about the slave trade and its cruelty. In the context of the age that introduced it, the Europeans employed cruelty until it lost its effect through common occurrence. It was an age when the macabre was so revered that cruelty was a spectacle of pleasure for most Europeans—a brigand, for example, would be purchased solely in order to see him tortured.[6] In their use of cruelty, Europeans made little racial distinction, as this account demonstrates:

> They [the indenture servants] are being bought and sold from one planter to another, or attached to horses and beasts for the debts of their masters, being whipt at the whipping post (as rogues) for their masters' pleasures, and sleeping in sties worse than hogs.[7]

What made the Africans more attractive, however, was their availability and sheer numbers from which Europeans could turn profits at unheard of rates.

John Hawkins opened the flow in 1562 in violation not only of Portugal's monopoly of the West African coast, but also of Spain's hegemony in the Caribbean. With great pride to the British, he unloaded his African cargo in Hispaniola for hides, ginger, sugar, and pearls. Hawkins' coup proved that mercantile expansions were as viable as their defenses. Spain, despite the wealth it was siphoning from the "New World," remained a relatively poor, obscurantist country incapable of defending its newfound riches. There were many political and geographical explanations for this incongruity. However, the most significant reason was that Seville, which the Spanish government had granted l'Exclusif right to trade with the Indies, was unable to provide for the colonies adequately. This fact, in tandem with the duties imposed by the Casa de Contracion, Seville's Trading House, on every purchase, resulted in widespread smuggling.

The Spanish colonists traded with all nationals regardless of flag. A letter to the king of Spain, dated May 20, 1563, from a colonial official demonstrates the friendly attitude of the colonists toward unlicensed trade:

> These people oppose justice here and bear a not friendly attitude toward me: because ever since I have arrived I have endeavored to enforce your Majesty's commands and royal cedulas particularly with respect to vessels which enter this port without manifests and are seized.[8]

If the monopolies on trade could be broken, regardless of the Pope's Bulls, so too could territorial hegemony. The king of France, Francis I, made the Gallic intention known as early as 1526 in this well-known statement:

> The sun shines on me as well as on others. I should be very happy to see the clause in Adam's will, which excluded me from my share when the world was being divided. God has not created those lands for Spaniards alone.[9]

Sir William Cecil, commenting on the Pope's Bull, stated to the Spanish ambassador to England, "the Pope had no right to partition the world and to take and give kingdoms to whomsoever he pleases."[10]

In this endeavor, Europe re-launched the scramble for the Indies. The European powers would war, sail, and maneuver in uncharted waters, first, to supply the Spanish colonials and later other colonists. And, as C. L. R. James vividly says: "... the slavers brought more and more Negroes, in numbers that leapt by thousands every year, until the drain from Africa ran into millions."[11] It was so, as this exclamation shows: "There are so many Negroes in this island [Hispaniola] as a result of the sugar factories, that the land seems an effigy or an image of Ethiopia itself."[12]

Spain's colonization and its methods were not lost; they, in fact, served as an example to the other European powers, which were gaining footholds in the region. The Spaniards continued to vary their own methods of expansion that later gave a national distinctiveness to their colonies. Half a century after England and France had won their "place in the sun" the character of Jamaica was hardly the same as that of St. Domingue.

Chapter One
The Birth of the French West Indies

France had resolved its internal religious strife with Henry IV's Edict of Nantes in 1598. In the years that followed, it set out to defy Spain whose navy had suffered an irreparable blow ten years earlier at the hands of the British. France and England, using the system of effective occupation, penetrated three areas where Spain had declared its sovereignty but had only sporadic contacts because her limited resources were too thinly spread. Those areas were North America, upper South America, and the Windward Islands.

French buccaneers used the coasts of Guadeloupe and Martinique, along with other nearby islands, to attack the Spanish flotillas and galleons on their voyages from Peru or Mexico to Castile. Spain tried repeatedly to take over the two main islands comprising Guadeloupe; however, the Caribs who had displaced the original Arawak inhabitants of Guadeloupe kept the Conquistadores at bay from the islands. Pierre Belain D'Esnambuc a pirate in the employ of Cardinal Richelieu then hounded Spain's forces from Guadeloupe's Grand-Terre in 1626. The Spaniards never returned. Cardinal Richelieu commissioned D'Esnambuc to take possession of Barbados and other islands in the region on behalf of the American Islands Co. (Compagnie des Isles d'Amerique), a trading syndicate.

The following document establishes the French empire in the Caribbean:

> We ... acknowledge and admit that we have formed and form by these presents a faithful association between ourselves to send an expedition, under the leadership of the Sieurs d'Esnambuc and du Rossey, Captains in the navy, or such others as we see fit to choose and name, to settle and people the Islands of St. Christopher and Barbados, and others situated at the entrance to Peru, from the eleventh to the eighteenth degree of the Equator, which are not in the possession of Christian princes, both to instruct the inhabitants of the aforesaid islands in the Catholic, Apostolic and Roman religion, and to trade and traffic in the products and merchandise which may be obtained and procured from the aforesaid islands and neighboring places, to bring them to France to Havre-de-Grace, in preference to all other ports, for the time and space of twenty years, and is more especially stipu-

> lated in the commission and authority which will be given to the said d'Esnambuc and du Rossey by My Lord Cardinal Richelieu, Grand-Master, Chief and Superintendent of French commerce.[1]

Full colonization of Guadeloupe and Martinique –"the others situated at the entrance to Peru" —began, however, only nine years later in 1635, when two of d'Esnambuc's lieutenants, Leonard de L'Olive and Jean Duplessis, landed and established the French colony of Guadeloupe. Later that year d'Esnambuc himself planted France's flag in Martinique.

According to the custom of the day, the state chartered companies to trade in or settle in, or both, specified areas with full ownership rights. There was, nevertheless, a corollary to these rights. Governments drew up articles to "instruct" the shareholders of such companies of their duties to the state. For example, Article IV of the American Islands Co.'s commission stated:

> They shall not admit to the islands colonists and settlements of any person who is not a Frenchman and who does not profess the Apostolic and Roman Catholic religion. If any other person should happen to enter the colony, he shall be forced to leave as soon as the governor of the island learns of it.[2]

This directive prescribed three mandated requisites: nationality, faith, and trade. The controls Spain had unsuccessfully tried to uphold, the French, the Dutch, and the British encouraged. Ignoring the lessons obvious in Spain's failure, they made war on each other not only in the Americas but also in Europe, Asia, and later Africa. (One legacy of this come and go struggle is that today people of the West Indies all speak a Creole tongue).

Article IV also presaged the level of insularity, which later befell Guadeloupe, Martinique, and later St. Domingue—France would be their only contact with the outside world. These policies began with Cardinal Richelieu. Prelate by profession, Richelieu was also a political leader with enormous dictatorial leanings. He founded French Absolutism, a system, which not only concentrated power in the person of the king and his bureaucrats; and notably for the West Indies, it centralized the political and administrative hands regulating France's colonies. Whereas the British planter could lobby Parliament or even buy a seat there, the planter in the French Caribbean did not enjoy the same privileges until later. To redress wrongs, the planter had to rely upon the impact colonial events had upon France itself. Lines were drawn very early in the life of the colonies. On one side of the Atlantic were the king, his secretary of the

Navy, and his governors. On the other side were the planter and his local council. The Atlantic was also the dividing line in terms of interests. France had the merchant, the company, and the capital lender. The colonies had the planter and the enslaved Africans.

Upon the death of Richelieu in 1642, another Cardinal succeeded to the reins of government. Also an absolutist, Mazarin's fiscal and centralizing policies provoked the rebellion of the Fronde. By the end of the rebellion in 1653 Mazarin's powers and policies became unquestioned to such an extent that upon Mazarin's death in 1661 his king, Louis XIV, could safely make the apocryphal statement, *I am the state (L'etat c'est moi).* Mazarin also bequeathed to Louis his deputy, Jean Baptiste Colbert, who, in a short time, became the central administrative figure in France and remained so until his death in 1683. Colbert brought French mercantilism to its zenith. His was not, however, the mercantile-bullionist system of Spain but, rather, a complex protectionist commercial arrangement geared toward positive trade balances.

France's mercantilist code was called *L'Exclusif,* but more aptly named *Colbertism;* and like the other proponents of mercantilism, it discouraged commerce with outsiders. Its "all roads lead to Versailles" rules reinforced the one-dimensional connection between colony and mother country. Nevertheless, the French, like other colonists in the Caribbean and elsewhere, survived because of illicit trade and even prospered despite disease, war and blockades. However, contraband declined once the British Navigational Acts removed the Dutch Free Traders from the area. Encouraged by governments and investors, fierce competition in production of sugar developed among planters in the various colonies. An overseer could easily boast, "though I have killed 30 or 40 Negroes per year, I have made my employer 20, 30, 40 or more hogsheads per year than any of my predecessors ever did."[3]

The competition within the Caribbean and for the benefit of the mother country has left its isolationist mark on the area. The people remain locked on a one-way street to France, unaware of their surroundings. "They," observe Eric Williams, "remain profoundly ignorant of the neighboring islands, each group basking in its special isolation."[4]

As in the case of Spain's Hispaniola, European laborers (called white slaves by the Dominican priest Jean-Baptiste Labat) voluntarily went to the French island colonies as *engagés* (contract laborers). On the other hand, the government summarily shipped them to the Caribbean in order to lessen unemployment in France. Prisoners could also do their sentence in the colonies always in search of laborers. In the eighteenth century,

Guyane became the major recipient of such migrants. As long as tobacco and cotton were the primary crops, the agricultural unit remained small, parceled-out farms needing few workers.

Tobacco and other previous crops required intensive cultivation but only small outlay for processing and labor. A family could economically run a farm with a few indentured servants. By contrast, sugar could be grown extensively with little expertise but was perishable and had to be processed immediately. A sugar factory required a heavy investment in buildings, machinery, and labor and continuous substantial supplies of raw cane; thus, sugar estates were much larger than the earlier farms.[5]

Once the *engagés* had served their thirty-six months, the company gave them a parcel of land to clear and seeds to grow a crop. These workers formed collective associations of two or three individuals and jointly worked their land holdings. However, two factors were to bring radical change to the nature of farming and the configuration of working units, not only in the French colonies, but also throughout the Caribbean. First, was the hegemony and quality of Virginia's tobacco over the Caribbean's; second, was the overwhelming demand for sugar in Europe and America.

With the emergence of sugar cane as a major crop, the demography and landscape of the Caribbean changed rapidly. The numerous small farms gave way to a few large estates—plantations. At the same time, comparatively cheaper captive Africans replaced European *engagés* whom the company had to remunerate in the form of wages after the thirty-six month contract period. Also worth noting was that European wars were depleting France of young men at the end of the seventeenth and beginning of the eighteenth centuries. In fact, the ordinance of April 8, 1699, forbade ship captains from taking on board any *engagés* under the age of eighteen.

Indissolubly linked to the expansion of French capital was the production of sugar—conceived as a multifaceted commercial undertaking whose benefits reached the smallest shopkeepers in France. Set in motion from Bordeaux, La Rochelle, Nantes, or Le Havre, ships of the Senegal Trading Company (*Compagnie du Senegal),* were loaded with French goods destined for the west coast of Africa. Once there, an eyewitness says, the French ships "worked" the coast from Dakar to Angola, including some of the coastal islands. From there the ships set sail for the French-controlled Caribbean islands, first stopping at Fort St. Pierre, Martinique, giving that colony first choice of the Africans. Planters paid "in raw sugar, indigo and the like, expressed in terms of weight."[6] The last leg of the triangular travel route called for the French ships, loaded with local produce, to return to France where raw sugar was refined for sale in Europe and resale in the colonies.

The enslavement of the African was the nexus in the alliance between sugar production and capital accumulation. The life and death of the slave were a major gear in this machinery. The more the colonies needed Africans, the more the slavers "worked" the west coast of Africa. Equally, the more ships there were in circulation, the more seamen, canvas, cordage, and like articles they used. They bred slaves in the American colonies, thus lessening the demands on Africa from that quarter. In the French Caribbean, this was not the case. Taking St. Domingue as an example, Eric Williams says, "Imports from 1764 to 1774 numbered 102,474. The slave population in 1776 was 290,000. Thus, despite an importation of over one hundred thousand, without taking into account the annual births, the increase of the slave population in thirteen years was less than 85,000."[7] The rule was "to work the slaves out, and trust for supplies from Africa."[8] One consequence of the degree of slave mortality was that newly arrived Africans were always present in the colonies. Not yet having been seasoned—trained to accept slavery, rebellion was high among them. Most of the revolts were African-led, with a sizeable number being exclusively tribal in nature.

In the seventeenth century, France continued to add to its empire. Concurrently with the beginning of the colonization of Guadeloupe and Martinique, a group of French settlers from Rouen, Normandy, established themselves on the Sinnary River (Guyane) in 1626, twenty-two years after France's first attempt at occupation. In 1635 another group settled on the island of Cayenne. These attempts at colonization were failures and the Dutch, who were already making inroads into neighboring territory, took up colonial residence in Cayenne. In 1664, Colbert had the Dutch evicted and Lefebvre de La Barre with some one thousand settlers revitalized the French colonization attempts of Cayenne. This last group was more successful but, from the beginning, Guyane acquired the reputation of being an unhealthy and difficult area to settle. Consequently, Guyane never received from France the attention given to St. Domingue, Guadeloupe, and Martinique. In addition, unlike those other colonies, the *engagé* system was not employed in Guyane, although the same farming pattern could be found there.

Also in the seventeenth century, France acquired the *de jure* proprietorship of the western third of Hispaniola in the 1697 Treaty of Ryswick. This area, re-named Saint Domingue, was not a new settlement. The de facto settlement of that colony had begun years earlier with the occupation by buccaneers stationed in the Cayman Islands and in Tortuga who preyed upon the Spanish galleons. The need to protect the fleet had compelled Spain to abandon the northern part of Hispaniola to reinforce Havana, a strategic port on the voyage to Seville. As in the case of Martinique and Guadeloupe, the French filled the void. Through the West Indies Co., (Compagnie des Indes Occidentales), the French authorities gave the buccaneers tracts of land to cultivate tobacco. Thirty-two years before the Treaty of Ryswick, these buccaneers, managed by France, founded the town of Port de Paix following their defeat at the hands of the British on Isla de Tortuga across the bay.

As they had done in Guadeloupe and Martinique, French centralism and exclusivity absorbed Guyane and St. Domingue into the fold of the French empire in the West Indies.

Chapter Two
Le Code Noir (The French Black Code)

Louis XIV promulgated the Code Noir in 1685. A compendium of laws and regulations, it remained the basic legal document by which France ruled the colonies for 163 years. The Code came from Colbert as a royal ordinance "concerning the Government, the Administration of Justice, the Police, the Discipline and the trade of Africans in the French colonies."[1] In the spirit of l'Exclusif, however, the Code added its own monopolies of religion, race, and sex.

The Code's first stipulations were on the subject of religion. The French did not want Protestants and Jews in the colonies. To enforce this rule, the Code insisted that only Catholics could own or be in charge of slaves who were to be baptized. The slaves could not be forced to work on Sundays or holidays, under penalty of confiscation of the owner's property. Marriage was permitted only between baptized slaves who had the consent of their masters. Newly arrived Africans, they placed under the tutelage of a baptized slave.

The children of slaves belonged to the owner of the mother thus ensuring their continued slave status. In the same vein, the status of children from the union of a slave and a freeman would depend on the status of the mother. However, Article IX prescribed a 2,000-pound of sugar penalty in cases of children born of a freeman and a slave.

Article XV of the Code forbade slaves from carrying arms of any type or assembling even for weddings. The slave who ran away for one month lost both ears and was branded on one shoulder. For a second offense, the buttocks were slashed and a brand placed on the other shoulder. The third time, death. A freed slave who gave shelter to a runaway was fined 3,000 pound of sugar a day; a freeborn, ten pounds a day. The slave, who struck a member of his owner's family and drew blood, would be put to death. The Code also prescribed severe penalty against the slave who struck any freeborn person.

According to Article XLII, owners could not punish a slave without cause. Mutilation or torture of slaves was forbidden under penalty of property confiscation and prosecution. If an owner or his agent killed a slave, the Code prescribed criminal prosecution.

Article XLIV declared the slave a *meuble* —movable property—that could be used as collateral. The slaves could not own property, could not hold public office, and could not bear witness in civil or criminal cases.

However, Article XLVII forbade the seizing or sale of family members separately if they were the property of one owner.

A number of articles prescribed the type of food and the amount the enslaved received weekly. The Code forbade giving rum instead of food on the slave's day off. Slaves not fed or clothed properly could report the infraction to the attorney-general who would take the matter before the court. Article LIV enjoined owners to be good fathers to their slaves and to take care of those who were old or infirm.

In the matter of inheritance, Article LVI decreed that the slave who became his master's heir was thenceforth free.

The final clauses of the Code (Articles LV-LX) pertained to the enfranchisement of the slave. After twenty years, a slave could be free. In addition, Article LIX gave the same rights, privileges, and immunities to freed slaves as to persons born free. However, Article LX enjoined the freed slave to be particularly respectful of their old masters, wives, and children.

Besides the aforementioned measures established to keep order, Article XLVIII also forbade, for example, the sale of slaves ages fourteen to sixty unless sold with the plantation where they lived. This was to ensure no disruption in sugar production. Such were the terms of the 1685 French Code Noir.

The Code was an unusually pragmatic set of rules designed to ensure maximum agricultural productivity from the colonies.[2]

The significant factor was that, France, by enacting the Code Noir, gave the slaves a semblance of legal protection against the white colonists. As a result, another line was drawn between slave and master in the French colonies, as blacks differentiated France from the planters; perceiving France and its representatives as more responsive to their plight than were the planters.

One result of the joint colonization of the West Indies by Africans and Europeans was the rise of the people of color. At the time of the introduction of Africans into the colonies, the government and the company did not look askance at their union with the whites. Until the introduction of the Code Noir in 1685, their offspring acquired the status of free men at birth. The colonists used them to amplify the number of whites that contract laborers and others from France were slow to increase. The Europeans accepted their interracial offspring because they were alarmed at the high ratio of enslaved Africans in the colonies. To be sure, the people of color did not have the benefits accorded a French citizen. In addition, when the white population increased and the army was settled in, the colored population's freedom withered. As masters, the whites did not care to share their privileges. Even the metropolitan government, which, in the beginning, had looked favorably upon miscegenation, recoiled when the colonists—restless under l'Exclusif—became more autonomy-minded. The government saw that the people of color would help the colonists challenge its authority. In 1778, for example, the Secretary of the Navy argued that "if, by means of such alliance, the whites ended reaching an understanding with the free people of color, the colony would easily be able to overthrow the king's authority and France would lose one of the most powerful links in its chain of commerce."[3] Marriage between the two groups was banned in order to militate against such an eventuality. The most significant result of this fear, however, was the declaration made on October 10, 1766, by the Secretary of the Navy stating that:

> All the Negroes have been transported to the colonies as slaves; slavery has imprinted an irremovable stain on their posterity; and consequently, those who come from it can never enter the class of whites. If ever the time came when they could be considered white, they would, like [the whites], claim all positions and dignities, which would be absolutely contrary to the constitution of the colonies.[4]

Whereas the metropolitan government across the Atlantic could only promulgate its wishes, the colonists, on the spot, could execute their stratagem to withhold privileges. The whites *balkanized* the people of color by dividing them into ten racial groups,[5] each group receiving its station in life according to its racial admixture.

These classifications had their roots in the relationship made between slavery and blackness. Race was the determinant, the explicit indication of one's position in society and in the division of labor. The slave was an African and black; the master was French and white. The acceptance of a color-coded deterministic system, either voluntarily or passively, underlies the basic infrastructure undergirding the colonies' living arrangement. It drew everyone into the vortex of an all-encompassing color syndrome. This system became everyone's raison d'être, to escape the mark that would tie one to the oblivion of slavery, which was itself tied to the land. Then occurred the French Revolution that sucked the oxygen out of the existent order in 1789.

Chapter Three
The 1789 French Revolution and Political Developments in The French West Indies

The French Revolution caused the collapse of the Old Regime, the various societies pulling from opposite ends in the colonies. The planters of St. Domingue, Guadeloupe, Guyane, and Martinique pulled to suspend l'Exclusif and establish free trade, restrain the colored population, and maintain slavery. The colored population looked to France for de facto equality with the white planters.

Article LIX of the Code Noir had decreed that freed men of color had the same rights, privileges, and immunities as the whites. However, the planters with the help of their associates in the mother country had chiseled away at the social guarantees enunciated in the Code. People of color were limited, for example, in the professions they could practice. However, they could be retail merchants and artisans, and, thus were able to buy property. The Code Noir banned only the slaves from owning property. By the time of the French Revolution, the freed men of color owned one-third of the estates and one-fourth of the slaves in St. Domingue alone.[1] The colored planters also participated in the commerce of l'Exclusif.

The wealthy people of color sent their children to France to be educated. While there, the students collaborated with a number of French philanthropists in founding the "Friends of the Blacks" pressure group that played the key role in putting the colored population's grievances on the Estates General's agenda. On April 4, 1792,[2] the Estates General elevated all free men of color to the rank of French citizens, and put them under the protection of the Rights of Men and of the Citizen that had been promulgated in 1789. This bill stated, in part, "that all citizens, equal before the law, are equally welcome to hold any public office without distinctions other than virtue and talent."

Events in the colonies followed events in France closely. At a time when ships traveling between France and Martinique took thirty-five days to cross the Atlantic, the rapid propagation of news from France to the colonies was remarkable. Sensing the end of their world, the partisans of the old order immediately attacked the partisans of the revolution. In Martinique, the planters, siding with the royalists, clashed with the businessmen, supporters of the bourgeoisie from the town of St. Pierre to whom they were heavily indebted. They were victorious at the Battle of Acajou on September 25, 1790.

Throughout the French colonies of the Caribbean, the revolution was characterized by pitched battles between the adherents of the white cockade, the royalists, and those of the tricolor. In St. Domingue, white planters defeated the men of color led by Vincent Ogé and Jean-Baptiste Chavannes in September 1790. One observer believed that the situation in the French colonies was exacerbated:

> by reformers of the ... day, who urging ... projects of amendment in the condition of human life, faster than nature allows, are lightning ... a consuming fire between the different classes of mankind.[3]

This observer further held that the rebellion of the [N]egroes in St. Domingo, and the insurrection of the mulattoes, to whom Ogé was sent as ambassador, had one and the same origin. It was not the strong and irresistible impulse of human nature, groaning under oppression, that excited either of those classes to plunge their daggers into the bosoms of unoffending women and helpless infants. They were driven into those excesses—reluctantly driven—by the vile machinations of men calling themselves philosophers (the proselytes and imitators of France, of the Old Jewry associates in London) whose pretences to philanthropy were as gross a mockery of human reason, as their conduct was an outrage on all the feelings of our nature, and the ties which hold society together![4]

The planters followed with repressive measures against the leaders of the rebellion, alighting a new phase in the war in St. Domingue between the white planters and the men of color. The news of Ogé's martyrdom commanded the full attention of Paris to the plight of the people of color, culminating in the decree of 1791 and 1792. To ensure the promulgation of its laws in the colonies, Paris sent commissioners to enforce them. In St. Domingue, the envoy was Leger Felicité Sonthonax, a man fiercely devoted to the revolution. The commissioners sent to Martinique, Guadeloupe, and Guyane pale in comparison. Then, also, in St. Domingue, Ogé's tortured death seems to have pointed to the necessity of collaboration between the men of color and the blacks[5] against the white planters.

Sonthonax's emancipation of the enslaved workers of St. Domingue on August 29, 1793, sent the whites to the barricades and into an alliance with the British forces led by Toussaint L'Ouverture defeated them. The National Convention heard of this on 16 Pluvoise An II (February 4, 1794) and "so deeply moved were the deputies that they took the almost unprecedented action of decreeing on the spot, without sending the matter first to committee, the emancipation of all slaves in the French colonies."[6] The French Revolution produced many such acts.

It was not all idealism, however.[7] The following year, Article VI of the Year III Constitution, established that "the colonies are an integral part of the Republic and are subject to the same constitutional laws." The revolution had turned the system on its head. Three years later, the law of 12 Nivose made the colonies departments (counties) of France. Representatives from the new French departments would now be included in the lower house of the legislature, the Council of the Five Hundred. With the exception of St. Domingue, the French Caribbean colonies are now Overseas departments of France (D.O.M.).

The revolution and the execution of Louis XVI in September 1793 provoked the formation of a general coalition of European monarchs led by England against France. Customarily, England and France either blockaded or occupied each other's colonies, until a treaty signing ceremony. England did this at the outset of the French Revolution. It occupied both Martinique and Guadeloupe, the former on March 23, 1794, the latter a month later. Martinique remained in British hands until 1802. As a result, the emancipation act of February 4 and the other principles of integration decreed by the French Legislative Assembly did not reach Martinique.

As to Guadeloupe, France retook it two months after the English occupation. It was the work of Commissioner Victor Hughes, who had gone to the Caribbean to announce that the people of Guadeloupe were free. With the help of most of the blacks in Guadeloupe, he defeated the British. The white planters and those of color who had supported the English were "terrorized" out of the island. Their lands were confiscated and "they fled by the thousands [to Martinique in British hands] to escape the revolutionary tribunal and death."[8] Thus was the racial make-up of Guadeloupe forever changed. The presence of fewer whites led to fewer mixed unions on that island.[9]

Victor Hugues remained the "special agent" in Guadeloupe for four years, during which time the blacks were the virtual rulers on behalf of the revolutionary French government. Two reactionaries, Jean Baptiste Raymond Lacrosse and Edme Étienne Borne-Desfournaux succeeded Hugues. The man of color, born a slave, Magloire Pélage, a veteran of America's war of independence, and his cohorts, overthrew Desfournaux and Hugues in a coup in 1801.

As 1802 dawned, Guadeloupe and St. Domingue had two former slaves at their helm: Pélage and L'Ouverture. In a proclamation addressed (in Creole) to "all the people of St. Domingue" the First Consul, Napoleon Bonaparte, reiterated the principles of the Declaration of the Rights of Man and of the Citizen, the Constitution of the Year III, and the Law of 12 Nivose (January 2). The proclamation read as follows:

> Of whatever color you may be, whatever your origin, we only want to know that you are all free, all equal before God and the Republic. During its revolution, France has known many misfortunes; while the whole world made war against it, the French fought against each other. But today all is finished, it's peace and reconciliation between Frenchmen; they all love the government and obey it. It is your turn people of St. Domingue; aren't *you French also*? Come to welcome those of your nation who are arriving; you will be happy to embrace your brothers and they will be happy to embrace you.[10]

There were doubts, however. Doubt on the part of the blacks that the forces led by Bonaparte's brother in law, General Charles Leclerc, were coming to impose slavery anew and doubt on the part of the French that the blacks would let Leclerc's forces succeed. Bonaparte, therefore, added to his proclamation, "do not believe those who tell you that the whites want to make slaves of you again; they lie. Remember, it is the Republic that gave you liberty and will maintain it. The soldiers [Leclerc's] are here to safeguard liberty and keep the country for the Republic."[11] Bonaparte sent the expeditionary forces, led by General Richepance, to Guadeloupe. Arriving in Pointe-a-Pitre on May 6, 1802, the General was welcomed by Magloire Pélage. In Basse-Terre, however, the men of color and the blacks, led by Louis Delgres and Joseph Ignace refused to lay down their arms. Pélage crushed Ignace's forces at Bainbridge on May 25. Ignace then killed himself. A few days later Delgres, surrounded by Richepance on the Anglemont habitation at Matoula, blew himself up with his men. There are reports that before the explosion, Delgres and approximately five hundred of his men held hands and shouted, *Point d'esclavage, vive la mort.*[12] (No more slavery, hooray for death.) On July 16, 1802, Richepance promulgated Bonaparte's decree re-establishing slavery and reinstituting the laws enforced in the colonies prior to the revolution. Slavery never abolished in Martinique because of the English occupation was simply maintained. St. Domingue turned its guns on Bonaparte's troops, defeating the expeditionary forces of Charles Leclerc and Donatien-Marie Rochambeaux in 1803. St. Domingue proclaimed its liberty and renamed itself Haiti in January 1804. In Guyane, which had 10,500 slaves to 1,300 whites at the outset of the Revolution,[13] slavery was reintroduced with the help of dogs. It also became a prison and grave for the political offenders of France, St. Domingue, and Guadeloupe. The stage was then set for the penal colony Bonaparte III established there in 1852. In Guadeloupe, some blacks continued to oppose the forces of Richepance as Maroons. However, the all-out resistance had collapsed with the defeats of Ignace and Delgres. What marked this island's history most during this period, however, was the repression against the insurgents by the returning émigrés. By the order of 22 Fructidor an X (9 September 1802) all blacks, including people of color, who claimed to have been free prior to 1789 were to report within three months to the prefect with documents proving status and property ownership. Failure to do so rendered them vagrants and subject to deportation. Until 1810 France promulgated countless decrees, ordinances, and orders to restrict the civil rights of free blacks as well as of people of color. The fears of the white planters seemed boundless. These repressive measures became as much a part of the history of French colonization, as were the social, political, and economic determinants such as the Code Noir, the Great Revolution of 1789, and l'Exclusif.

Chapter Four
France and the Spirit of Integration

The Bonaparte regime rejected the effort of the revolution concerning the integration of the colonies. That was particularly true of Article VI of the Year III Constitution making the colonies an integral part of France and subject to French laws. Bonaparte's constitution of 22 Frimaire, Year VIII, declared the law null and void and decreed that France would govern the colonies through separate laws.

The spirit of integration did not perish, however, with the coming of Bonaparte. Too much of that spirit derived from cultural and historical "conditioning," symbolized by the new republic, achieved through demands for equality in the course of making a revolution. As Raymond Betts points out, "Bonaparte's colonial policy was the result of practical concerns, not doctrinal ones."[1]

Concerning the assimilation of the colonies as departments of France and the extension of citizenship to its people, one should recall the correlation the French have made between their own ancestors, the Gallo-Romans and the colonized, and between France and Rome.

Every French child learns that Julius Caesar defeated the brave but barbarian Gauls in 52 B.C. at Alesia. The French child is inculcated with pride at the adoption his ancestors made of the civilization, the language, and the religion of the conquering Romans. The Gauls intermarried with the Romans and, indeed, became Gallo-Romans. Because of the domination of Rome, the French child learns that his ancestors were considered the most civilized people in Europe. The Latin of the Roman soldiers replaced the Gauls' Celtic tongue, and Rome's monuments, laws, literature—all were copied, and ultimately adopted. Finally, in 211, the edict of Caracalla made the Gauls Roman citizens.

The French have indeed been imbued with what can be termed the "Roman complex." From the Gallic poet Rutilus Namasianus to the historian Michelet, they all have sung the praise of Rome. The absorption with the Roman part of their heritage led the French not only to develop the Code Bonaparte, known as the modern Roman civil law, but also to set themselves up as the inheritors of what they perceived to be the *mission civilisatrice* (civilizing task) of the Romans toward the barbarians.

The different attitudes displayed by France toward the people who have passed through its rule set lasting stereotypes. The Africans were the barbarians devoid of culture, to be manipulated and coaxed into civilization while the Asiatics were held in wonder.[2] Middle Easterners were distrusted, while Polynesians were amusing.

If the Latin part of their heritage instilled in them the Roman assimilationist political outlook, what role did their Catholicism whose origin was also Roman play in the colonization of Martinique, Guadeloupe, St. Domingue, and Guyane? Catholic orders such as the Dominicans, the Carmelites, the Capuchins, the Brothers of Charity, and the Jesuits bought Africans just as any planter did. The Jesuits in 1763, the year of their expulsion from the colonies, had more than three hundred Africans in slavery in Guadeloupe alone.[3] The Church of Christ did not condemn the enslavement of Africans until the second half of the nineteenth century. Indeed, preached St. Paul to Philemon, God was acquiescent to slavery against which any revolt was an impious act. St. Thomas expounded this St. Augustine's theme into a patriarchal order. It is the Catholic Church's influence, which, in the end, had the greatest impact on colonial societies. For, whereas a Protestant stands as an individual and indeed received his salvation by going against the grain, a Catholic who protests is condemned. The Church rejected the protesting Catholic and looked upon him as a threat no different from the Maroon, the captive African who had freed himself. Submission was the mark of a pious Catholic society, and in a colonial context, piety became obedience to the colonial situation itself. The black man, from the Christian point of view, had to participate in his enslavement or as Sartre has said, "share in the responsibility of a crime of which he was the victim"[4] since his salvation for being African was in the very enslavement which provided him with Christianity.

The schematic result was that the French Catholic Church, which the Code Noir had given the monopoly of religion in the colonies as early as 1685, cemented the French colonial policies at the grass roots by its submissiveness promoting rules. As the age of emancipation dawned, it was clear that France had introduced more than armed forces to uphold its sovereignty over the colonies. In fact, these other forces proved far more powerful than Bonaparte's armies did.

The loss of St. Domingue, its most prosperous colony, dealt a crippling blow to France's American empire. Compounded by the handicap that slavery had become on its industrial sector plus mounting rebellions in the colonies, France, surreptitiously at first, let it be known that the metropolitan government favored abolition.

The fortune of the abolitionists in France and the colonies followed closely the republic's fate. The enslaved Africans' desire for emancipation and the people of color's agitation for equality preyed on the tribulations and conflicts between royalists and republicans throughout the nineteenth century. At the same time, Jacobins, the revolutionary front battling for the enactment of a republic, enflamed the spirit of emancipation in the colonies. The royalists influenced the planters in a similar way.

Some historians believe that Bonaparte declared the slave trade illegal following his escape from Elba, as a way of swaying the British in his favor. Louis XVIII rescinded the declaration only to proclaim himself, in 1815, the end of the slave trade in the colonies. The trade, however, continued until France abolished slavery in April 1848 following Great Britain, which had done so in 1833. This last phase of the slave trade was particularly arduous for the Africans who were caught in the desperate voracity of slavers facing the end of an epoch of lucrative profits.[5] The king, who had himself proclaimed the end of the trade in 1815, reminded the governor of Guadeloupe in an 1823 memo that, "the social system [in the colonies] rests on particular foundations adapted to the necessities that caused them to be adopted. It admits legal slavery and thus enfranchisement; it also admits distinction in the status of persons, according to the classes of the population to which they belong."[6] Moreover, the king further reminded his governor of the purpose for which the colonies were created: "The colonies situated in the West Indies have for principal purpose to furnish consumers for French products and to produce for France exotic goods ... and to open markets where France does not have to fear neither competition nor foreign government regulations."[7] Thus, despite the overwhelming evidence that both slavery and l'Exclusif had become serious burdens for the colonies, the French government still chose to maintain both. The major reason for this contradiction was the huge profits France derived from the institution of slavery and from the trade in slaves, which France had, a priori, exclusive rights in its colonies.[8]

The abolition of slavery began in earnest with the rebellions of the blacks and the men of color in the colonies. Throughout Martinique in 1822, 1831, and 1833 uprisings occurred against the planters. Soon after the British relinquished Martinique and Guadeloupe to French authority, free men of color, despite the planters' objections, began to return home.[9] Did they bring back views of a wider world? Undoubtedly! Censored pamphlets denouncing inequality, such as *The Fate of the People of Color in the French West Indies* found their way to the colonies. The government responded with sporadic edicts against such infractions.

However, in 1830 the government enacted several laws regarding the status of the people of color, abolishing laws depriving the free men of color of their citizenship rights. The procedures for manumission were simplified, and France became the automatic granter of freedom to any enslaved person who touched its soil. It is no coincidence that these laws, which were extensively debated in the legislature, passed at the time of the July 1830 Revolution that overthrew Charles X and the "ultra-reactionary" Villele cabinet. A bourgeois-royalist compromise established the "July Monarchy" of Louis-Philippe who would end both the monarchy in France and slavery in the colonies. On February 9, 1927, the government issued an ordinance creating a general council in each colony, and the post of deputy to the National Assembly in Paris. There followed countless other ordinances and laws, culminating in the law of March 19, 1946, conferring the status of *Départements* (counties) upon Guyane, Guadeloupe and Martinique.

In France, the period of clamor against slavery was also the age of the arguably most renowned artistic school in France—Romanticism. In its ranks were poets such as Lamartine (Alphonse Marie Louis de Prat de Lamartine) who, as politicians, proclaimed the abolition of slavery and affixed their names to the emancipation act itself.

Chapter Five
Abolition—View by Victor Schoelcher

Victor Schoelcher was one the Romanticists. His fanatical zeal made him stand out among all the men from the Society for the Abolition of Slavery pressure group who toiled against slavery. Schoelcher had an indefatigable pen, which he used to weave a web of reasons as to why France should abolish slavery. In his book, *The Abolition of Slavery*, he also contested the allegation that Africans had no civilization, taking as proof the data René Caillé had discovered on his 1828 expedition to Timbuktu.[1] Regarding the status of the colonies, Schoelcher's views prevailed in the struggle against slavery he and his colleagues waged during the February 1848 Revolution.

Schoelcher was as much against l'Exclusif as he was a firm believer in the policy of assimilation and integration of the colonies within France. In that regard, he said the following:

> We do not belong to the political school of big money. We hate the doctrines of the 17th century's statesmen; whatever the colonies cost or do not cost to France, we love them; we do not want to separate from them, and we will always defend them because they are French. It is monstrous to say, the colonies having been instituted for the benefits of the metropole, the advantage of the metropole must prevail to the detriment of all colonial interests.[2]

Schoelcher then underlined the major reason France should keep its West Indies colonies. He wrote:

> ...The [C]reoles are not a conquered people, the colonies are not conquered countries, but really lands peopled by our parents and our fellow countrymen who went to establish themselves there under the common pact. At least a quarter of the island's white population is made of French Europeans, the rest of French colonists. To deal with the possible abandonment of Guadeloupe and Guyane or the abandonment of the Vosges and Central departments is to us one and the same...the people of Martinique are as French as the people of [France].[3]

In the following years, in France and in the colonies they debated this view. In 1946 it became law. Thus of all the French colonies, only the *colonies de peuplement,* the settler colonies—Algeria, Reunion,

Guadeloupe, Guyane and Martinique—became French departments. Senegal did not miss by much.[4]

As 1848 approached and as more and more groups[5] joined in the clamor for the abolition of slavery, the question then raised was: Should

Statue of Victor Schoelcher freeing a slave in front of the old courthouse in Fort de France Martinique. Born in Alsace, Schoelcher initiated the April 27, 1848 decree abolishing slavery in France and its colonies.

abolition be gradual or immediate? Since their victory over the French in June 1815, the British had been pressuring them to end the slave trade. The British had adopted a system of apprenticeship in their colonies before complete emancipation. This impressed the French abolitionists, and they would have proposed the same for the French colonies had the masses in Paris and the slaves in the colonies not taken matters into their own hands with the revolution of 1848.

With the news that on February 14, Parisians had revolted and established the Second Republic, the slaves of St. Pierre in Martinique set fire to plantations, forcing Governor Rostolan to proclaim the immediate abolition of slavery. By March 4, the revolution had provided Schoelcher the opportunity to convince[6] the Minister of War and the Navy, François Arago, to make two essential decisions. First, sign a preparatory decree ordering the abolition of slavery; second, create a special commission—under the direction of Schoelcher—charged with the writing of the final decree ordering the immediate emancipation in all of the Republic's colonies. The official decree was finalized on April 27, 1848. Before Governor Laryle in Guadeloupe knew of the decree, however, he had found it necessary to proclaim the immediate emancipation on May 27. The general commissioner arrived in the colonies with the official proclamation in June. With the abolition of slavery, the Republic, as it had done in 1794, decreed the blacks to be French citizens. The Republic also decreed, for the first time, the universal suffrage for all male citizens twenty-one and over.

The revolution of 1848, led by members of the Romantic School, radicalized the political system not only in the colonies but also in France. The colonists could now elect three deputies to the National Assembly in Paris. In addition, for the first time since the 1790s, the people of the colonies—within the confines of the French Republic—had a voice in the passage of laws governing their lives.

However, the Second Republic immediately ran into difficulties on the economic front. How was the government to compensate the planters for the loss of their slaves? It never contemplated compensating the former slaves. After much debate between the planters and the commissioners, the government decreed that it would pay 425.34 francs per slave in Martinique which had a total slave population of 74,447 as of March 1848; 469.53 francs in Guadeloupe which had had a slave population of 87,087;74 and 618 francs in Guyane.[7] Then too, it was decided, even before the act of abolition was drafted, that the colonies would have to import indentured laborers. The decree of February 13 and March 23, 1852, instituted the contracted laborer act, which continued officially until 1887. Figures vary greatly as to the actual number of Africans, Indians, Chinese, and Annamese (Vietnamese) who immigrated to Guyane, Guadeloupe, and Martinique. Overall, it is believed that approximately 24,000 Africans, 115,000 Indians, 2,000 Chinese, and 750 Annamese went to the French West Indies. This was as wasteful a system as slavery. In Guyane, for example, Eric Williams notes, "whereas the man-days worked numbered 26,852 the man-days lost in the hospital were 26,602. The average number of days worked by each immigrant was twelve per month—for every day worked, one day was spent in the hospital."[8]

Then, the political gains of the Second Republic disappeared with the advent of Napoleon III.[9] In February 1852, universal suffrage and parliamentary representation were once more disallowed in France and its colonies. There, the General Council operated at the pleasure of Napoleon III's representative. The newly manumitted black population's freedom was restricted, and passes and poll taxes became the order of the day.

The economic sector also quickly changed from the feudal to the modern during this period. Until then, the planter seldom invested in the improvement of his means of production. However, the growth of the sugar beet industry, whose production the French encouraged when the English blockaded France's Caribbean colonies at various times during the Napoleonic wars, was by 1830 already one-eighth the colonial sugar production. The French government's use of surtaxes and other protectionist measures compounded the threat from sugar beet production. Supported by French capital, these negative measures resulted in the concentration (particularly in Guadeloupe which had lost a greater number of local planters in the 1790s) of landed property and farming stocks into the hands of the major colonial manufacturers.[10] The introduction in the 1850s of French banks in the colonies finalized this process. In 1860 Napoleon III gave the deathblow to l'Exclusif trading system by opening the doors of his colonies to British commerce. However, in the end, the sugar industry of Guadeloupe, Guyane, and Martinique could not compete with the growing technology of either European beet sugar production or Cuba's vast sugar cane industry.

International competition in the sugar industry reached crisis levels in the 1880s. The subsequent fall of prices bankrupted many independent sugar factory owners. In Guadeloupe, many sold out to French joint stock companies and in Martinique to the richer planters, resulting in a greater concentration of land in the hands of the wealthy white Creoles. By 1965, 89 percent of Martinique's and 96 percent of Guadeloupe's export came from the lands owned by the wealthy whites.[11]

Chapter Six
The Assimilation of the Colonies

The defeat of Napoleon III at the hands of the Prussians opened the door to the Third Republic on September 4, 1870. With the return of the Republic, the war between Royalists and Republicans ended—the Royalists having finally abandoned the field. The men of 1848, particularly the indomitable Victor Schoelcher, were present to reimpose universal male suffrage and representation of the colonies in the French parliament. The 1875 constitution provided two seats for deputies and one for a senator from each colony. The Third Republic extended French laws to Guyane, Guadeloupe, and Martinique making these colonies, even at that time, virtual counties of France.

Unmistakable developments marked France's growing absorption of the colonies. For example, France extended to them the 1884 right of workers to organize; it modernized colonial municipalities at the same time it did at home; it established in that decade the jury system in its Caribbean colonies; it extended the draft to men from the colonies in 1911 and placed a customs board in the colonies in 1924.

In regards to education, there were a number of elementary schools prior to 1880. Catholic congregations ran these schools, primarily for the benefit of the planters. And a few, called mutual teaching schools, came into prominence in the 1820s to educate the children of the wealthy people of color. In 1851, the governor general opened an alternate school system for whites and children of color to attend a secondary school in France.[1] There were no schools for free or enslaved black children until 1882. However, it was the opening of the non-clerical public schools in the 1880s that had after the above mentioned Catholic Church the most influential and far-reaching impact on French colonization in the West Indies.

The conflict between the republic and the Catholic Church, ally of the Royalists, found its battlefield in the French schools. Until 1882, the Church controlled primary and secondary education in France. Half of the boys and all of the girls in France attended Catholic parochial schools.[2] Increasingly, to a growing number of Republicans, Catholic education stood as a threat to the republican equalitarian way of life.[3] By dint of a series of laws passed by the Jules Ferry government in 1880, the Catholic orders were put out of the business of teaching in the French public schools. At the same time, the law of June 16, 1881, made education free, and the law of March 28, 1882, made elementary education compulsory. However, the government made no provision until 1946 to assist parents in the colonies in sending their children to elementary school. Education was, from the very beginning, of an elitist orientation, made more so by the competitive entrance examinations for the French Civil Service. The government did provide extensively for scholarships to the secondary schools—the Lycées—and for further studies at the university and at the Colonial Administration School, both in France.[4]

Traditionally the school carries on as nationalism's cradle and the grounding catalyst of acculturation. It was at the school bench that French colonization had its success assured in the French West Indies and Guyane. Had it been left to the planters to decide the fate of education in the colonies, only they would have enjoyed its fruits. In countless letters to the governors, the planters expressed their fears of educating blacks. France perceived the issue differently. Education was an integral part of its civilizing mission. Bordeaux, which had been the major French town in the triangular trade, became the center of education for all the French colonies. And, until 1973, curricula and major exams given in the colonies were planned there. The curricula were steeped in the metropolitan tradition of classical education in which Latin, French, and French History are the major subjects. These curricula fit with the predominant French notion that Africans and their descendants were *tabula rasa* or blank slates whom France had a duty to impregnate with its culture. History was a subject wherein France found the opportunity to show itself in the best light; and Africa, when not projected as a barbaric continent, was depicted as an "extension of Western conquest."[5] For example, French Occidental Africa's Governor General Roume, when speaking about educational reform, stated in 1924,

> All the teachings of history and geography must show that France is a wealthy, powerful nation capable of making herself respected. France is also great because of the nobility of her sentiments and her generosity. She has never retreated from sacrificing men and money to deliver people from enslavement or to provide savage populations with peace, and the benefits of civilization.[6]

The students who had successfully passed the baccalaureate and wished to study for a career other than elementary school teachers had, until 1970, to travel to France. This trip to the mother country climaxed the elitist course in the assimilationist educational system. Going to France was intended to immerse the colonial student in the bosom of French culture and then return him as a model to the colonies. Consequently, a Guadeloupean could shout in 1936, "Vive la France," upon seeing the black governor, Felix Eboué, who found the correlation "beautiful and was moved by it."[7] This was the "Golden Age" of assimilation.

In 1909 a decree that would have joined the "old colonies" of Reunion, Guyane, Guadeloupe, and Martinique to the mother country as Overseas Departments of France was drafted but because of the First World War never implemented. At the end of the war, to which the French West Indies had sent more than 35,000 men—23,000 were wounded, killed, or taken prisoner—assimilation as a French policy reached a dead end. (During the 1862 Mexican adventure of Napoleon III and Maximilian, France had also sent a contingent of volunteers from Guadeloupe and Martinique to Mexico.) A new policy, muted from the old, had began to take shape as early as 1881 when the "union" of the "Algerian public services to the various French ministries" was enacted.[9] That policy was equality status for the settler-colonies of Guyane, Reunion, Algeria, Guadeloupe, and Martinique. Equality meant making them *Départements*, counties, local administrative units of the French state. This new policy of equality reached full bloom during the Popular Front's socialist-communist concordat in 1936–1938. (What also became clear during the regime of the Popular Front was that France's policy of assimilation would be turned into the policy of association in the French colonies of Africa).

World War II is remembered in Martinique and Guadeloupe as *the time of Admiral Robert,* which translates as one of the most difficult periods in recollection to those who endured it.

The capitulation of French forces and the subsequent armistice in June 1940 brought to the colonies Vichy's authoritarian regime, represented by Admiral Georges Robert. Colonial politics came to a halt. Then, too, the entrance of the U.S. into the war meant the blockade of France's Caribbean colonies. Provisions and supplies from France could not get through. The rationing of bread and meat strained relations between French sailors and the black population. The sailors conducted themselves as an army of occupation and appropriated the lion's share of the available food supply. Some overtly advocated Hitlerism and repressed the black population. Guyane fared better, as few Frenchmen cared to go there. Guyane was also less populated and did not have the same difficulties with food supplies as Martinique and Guadeloupe.

The black population vividly contrasted General Charles De Gaulle's Free French movement to the Vichy regime in power. Frantz Fanon, in Martinique during this period, explained that to the black population, De Gaulle represented the true France, which the sailors had betrayed.[10] The event was reminiscent of 1789. Then the people of color contrasted the revolution's principles with the planters' ideology. Although this period lasted but three years, it was most influential in giving De Gaulle god-like status in the colonies, putting the colonies squarely behind his parties, the R.P.F., Rassemblement du Peuple Francais, and the Union pour la Nouvelle République (U.N.R.).

In the flush of triumph after the war, the Fourth Republic's Constituent Assembly voted, on March 19, 1946, law number 46–451 classifying as French counties, Guadeloupe, Martinique, Reunion, and Guyane. Article 2 added, "the laws and decrees presently in force in France and which are not yet being administered in these colonies will be, before January 1, 1947, applicable to these new counties." In the same vein, Article 3 stated that "immediately after the promulgation of this present law, all new laws applicable to France will also be applicable to these counties unless specified otherwise." With this ultimate decree in France's absorption arsenal, the roughly 311 years of colonization culminated with Guyane, Guadeloupe and Martinique becoming—hypothetically—integral parts of France. Paris replaced the governor with a prefect; the colonial roads became "national roads;" the public services, the judiciary and the police became extensions of France's own. In 1959 the Ministry of Overseas Departments and Territories (D.O.M.T.O.M.) replaced the Ministry of the Interior, which, until that time, had authority over the colonies. The change of ministries has been the only major recognition by France that Guadeloupe and Martinique are 7,000 and Guyane 10,000 kilometers across the Atlantic. In 1960, the locally elected General Council that had until then held an advisory position vis-à-vis the governor and prefect was given finance and legislative oversight in their respective county (*département*). As part of the continuing policy of departmentalization, a French West Indian university, whose major campus is located in Guadeloupe, opened its doors in the 1970s.

One measure of the neglect Guyane has suffered since its French colonial founding is the scarcity of archival and other materials relating to its history. However, thanks to France's administrative centralism, one may follow Guyane's evolution in the overall context of France's colonial policies in the Caribbean.

What has marked Guyane most was the penal colony that France created at Saint-Laurent-du-Maroni in 1852. With the vague notion of providing white labor to a mismanaged colony, Europeans knew little of its geography and climate. The prisoners, later immortalized in René Belbenoit's novel, *Dry Guillotine,* had to spend by law a double prison term in the colony. Sentenced to remain in Guyane the length of time spent in prison, it was not uncommon for four out of seven to die yearly,[11] or to be so broken at the end of their first sentence as to be useless to the colony.[12] But inevitably, they further increased the racial mixture of the coastal Guyanese.

Unlike the plantations in St. Domingue, Guadeloupe, and Martinique, those in Guyane generally were small. Thus, when gold was discovered in 1855, the labor drain doomed the plantations to return to the Inini jungle. Gold lured prospectors of all nationalities to Guyane; it also was the cause of border clashes with Brazil. To resolve their differences, France, through the arbitration of the Swiss, gave up 260,000 square kilometers of Guyane's territory to Brazil, reducing the colony to an area of approximately 92,000 square kilometers between the Oyapock and Maroni Rivers,[13] making it the smallest political unit in South America and the only non-independent one there.

In 1974, to underline the unique relationship France has had with its Caribbean colonies since the seventeenth century, they were, in addition to départements, given the status of French regions, the prefects serving both departmental and regional functions. Locally based regional councils have limited financial and legislative powers over the "Regions."

Chapter Seven
Interaction of Peoples and Races in the French-speaking Caribbean

In the French West Indies, the people who came from France and the people brought from Africa, along with their offspring, built a society at the center of which toiled the enslaved. Blackness, which characterized the slave and slavery, became the overt *primum mobile* from which positions in society were determined. Underneath color, a culture evolved from the African-slavery–European-master model that produced the dynamics through which France was assured the dominant status in St. Domingue, Guyane, Guadeloupe, and Martinique.

The white groups: Creoles and French

White society in the colonies was not a monolithic unit, but was stratified along economic and racial lines. Nationality was a security valve the planters could easily discard when necessary to safeguard their interests and positions through other means. For example, the planters of St. Domingue invited the British to take over the island during the French Revolution. Like the *émigrés* fleeing the 1789 Revolution, they found it more advantageous to have their patrimony in foreign hands than lose their privileges.

The white community consisted of three main groups. First, there were the *engagés* (the contract laborers) whose descendants had become small farmers or artisans. Second, there were the non-propertied government officials. Third, there were the large plantation-slave owners. Only those whose families had lived in the colonies for many generations were considered Creoles.

The first group often referred to as *petit blanc* or *beké goyave* (in Martinique) and *petit habitant* (in Guyane) could be compared to the poor whites of the United States. They were the descendants of the thirty-six month labor contractors who had toiled in the tobacco and sugar cane plantations. The limited land mass of the islands soon restricted the policy of donating land to these indentured servants at the completion of their service to the charter company. In addition, the replacement of tobacco with sugar cane farming, which required large plantations and capital, doomed the *petit blanc,* the small whites, at first to be vegetable farmers and artisans, then petty bureaucrats. Overwhelmingly, their occupation later was that of overseer and general employees for their richer brethren. Lacking economic independence and education, they valued above all the color of their skin.[1] Throughout the history of the French colonies in the Caribbean and circum-Caribbean, the *petits blancs*, justly insecure, thought themselves threatened by the people of color. As a result, they "were largely responsible for the clamor which arose against miscegenation."[2] This group of white Creoles cared little about education beyond the mandatory age, nor did they have the means whether economic or social to provide one for their children.[3] They seldom, if ever, conversed in French, and it was generally believed they never visited the mother country that their ancestors had left in the seventeenth and eighteenth centuries. Consequently, they filled the significant function of the culturally deprived model in a colonial system of the assimilationist type. They provided a gauge against which blacks could measure the level of French culture necessary for their own self-image. In the socialization or assimilation process, the small whites have represented, therefore, who one should not culturally be. The small whites, despite the often-exploited position they have held since the inception of the colonies, could not envision a status post. Where else would their race and color in relation to their economic status, culture, and education give them any viability? Not in France! Like the Afrikaner of old, they had no other place to go and as such were the "real partners of the colonized, because it was they who had the most need of colonial compensation and life ... They had bet everything and forevermore on the colonies."[4] To sustain themselves as Creoles, the small whites had, therefore, allied their limited interests with the vastly superior ones of the richer whites of whom they were the political and economic victims.[5]

In songs, the second group of colonial whites often is referred to as "Metropolitans" or *oiseux de passage,* migratory birds. Because of their transitory status in the colonies, they seldom became one of the upper-class whites.

With the new status of *department* conferred in 1946, a wave of French civil servants and tourists flooded Guadeloupe and Martinique. Until then, the metropolitans had been mostly military men and government officials of various categories whose occupations were to supervise and maintain the interests of their home country in the colonies. This group left France, as Albert Memmi notes, because "...one gets paid more and spends less. One goes to the colonies because positions are assured, salaries high, careers advance faster and businesses are more fructuous."[6]

Except for Guyane, which was shunned and where an official's tour of duty often was regarded as a form of banishment, the metropolitans followed the mythical call to the exotic isles where their skin color had greater value.

As centuries of colonization succeeded one another, the metropolitan became the true colonizer. Neither the small whites nor the large plantation owners could claim this status, mainly because they had themselves been socialized and assimilated into the West Indian modus vivendi. The wealthy Creoles, after generations of island or Guyanese life, in time, adopted many of the slave culture's ways. As such, in spite of the master slave relationship that existed prior to 1848 plus the system instituted afterward to safeguard the wealthy Creoles' dominant status, the wealthy Creoles were "in this together" with the other permanent residents of the colonies. Whereas the wealthy Creoles represented perennial domination to the blacks, the metropolitans were neither permanent nor perceived as tormentors. The metropolitans only transited in the colony. Moreover, the metropolitans often looked on the colonies with the inner detachment of the powerful or of the outsider; and displayed a paternalistic attitude toward the blacks, whom many regarded as epitomizing Rousseau's "Noble Savage;" unlike the wealthy Creoles, who, fearing the "black hordes," relied on a brutal racist ideology and attitude to suppress them. This is not to say that the metropolitan was free of racist attitudes. Theirs was, however, more of the expedient than of the dogmatic type. To be sure, they represented metropolitan interests, which sometimes were contrary to the planters'; and in the colonial context that meant being more responsive to black demands. Consequently, segments of the black population in Guadeloupe and St. Domingue always supported the French government when called to defend the colonies against the planters, Great Britain, and Spain.

The metropolitans who succeeded each other in their tours of duty in the French colonies of the Caribbean brought with them the latest in fashion, literature, and ideas from a France, which the world generally regarded as liberal. Not yet having to contend with a large population of another race or religion on their soil, the French exalted in humanistic principles, which were often contrary to the interests of the maritime bourgeoisie.

At the apex of the colonial pyramid dwelled the *grands blancs, grans békés,* the wealthy white Creoles. Enriched by slavery and sugar cane, this subgroup of Creoles (who had earlier wanted to swell their number through interracial unions only to cast out their offspring later on) walled themselves with their privileges against all other groups. Moreau de Saint-Mery, a wealthy Creole, chronicled extensively French colonial life during most of the eighteenth century.

In his *Topographical, Civic, Political, Historical Description of the French Part of the Island of St. Domingue*, Saint-Mery observed that the wealthy Creole lived in an exaggerated opulence, which astounds the Europeans. The crowds of slaves who await orders or even signals from just one man give a sense of importance to whoever commands them. A wealthy man owes it to himself to have four times as many servants as he needs.[7]

His children learned early the master's dictatorial mores:

> Put among little slaves who are condemned to obey his slightest whim or, what is even more revolting, to suppress all of their own, he will not tolerate the least opposition. No despot has had more attentive homage, no more constant adulators than the child of the wealthy planter. Each slave is subjected to the fluctuations of his temper, and his childish tantrums only too often trouble domestic tranquility, for he can command any injustice his ungovernable will desires.[8]

The character of the wealthy Creole woman did not escape de Saint-Mery's sharp pen. Used to dominating, she was another scourge slaves had to contend with. "Nothing," says he "equals the temper of a wealthy Creole woman punishing the slave whom her husband has perhaps forced to sully the conjugal bed."[9] And, concurrently,

> There is no widow who, despite her affection for her children, does not soon erase by a new marriage the name and memory of the man whom she seemed to have loved so desperately. Perhaps there is no other country where second marriages are as common as in St. Domingue, and women are to be seen there who have had seven husbands.[10]

The wealthy planter also cared obsessively about appearances, and his class concerned itself ostentatiously with its members' ancestral origins. Often acting the would-be gentleman, he constantly reminded himself of the following caveat: "One must keep one's origin secret when it is not a noble one, and for some envious person who found it out in the mother country to reveal the truth is indeed too much to bear."[11] If the wealthy Creole's search for titles of nobility were the stuff of Moliere's comedic plays, doubt about his racial purity, no matter how many generations removed, was akin to a Shakespearean tragedy. A rumor of blackness among one's ancestors was a wealthy Creole's ultimate misfortune. In his novel, *La Caldeira*, Raphael Tardon, relates the story of such a rumor about de Saint-Mery. In this excerpt, de Saint-Méry's wife herself doubts him and opens the door to an imagination filled by centuries of dogmatic racism.

> There isn't smoke without fire, concluded Athenais. I would then have been for eight years the wife of a man of color, and my son carries in his veins a bit of impure blood. Everybody will know it. What have you done? ...In her frame of mind she saw hallucinating images of Negroes with ferocious pictures of the saber tooth tiger, spitting hate.[12]

Regarding interracial relationships, it was anathema for a wealthy Creole woman of whatever status to be involved with a man of color. It was less repulsive, however, for a wealthy white man to be involved with a black woman as long as he did not contemplate anything legal.

Like the ruling-class white Creole, both the metropolitan and the *petit blanc* practiced endogamy in the colonies. The *petit blanc* was ostracized at social events, except at funerals when he was allowed to pay his respects to his richer brethren who had never invited him inside his home. So fearful were the wealthy whites of losing their remaining footholds in Guadeloupe and Martinique that consanguineous marriages were not infrequent among them. Edith Kovats-Beaudoux says of the wealthy white Creoles' dilemma that:

> Numerous marriages between wealthy white Creoles and colored people would soon end in the dismantling of the group as a racial entity. Similarly, frequent unions with Metropolitans or foreigners would result, notably through the mechanism of inheritance, in a perceptible dispersion of wealth toward the outside world and simultaneously in an increasing control of Beké assets by foreign elements.[13]

The wealthy white Creoles, too, have suffered setbacks during the centuries of colonization. During the Haitian war of independence, for example, those who did not leave the island were virtually exterminated and later forbidden by the Dessalines constitution to own property in Haiti. In Guadeloupe, the regime of Victor Hugues and Magloire Pelage expelled the majority of Creoles who had been partisans of the white cockade against the French Revolution. Although many returned, their number never again reached the level prior to the revolution.

In Guyane, the abandonment of agriculture in favor of mining, after the discovery of gold in 1855, and the opening of the penal colony at St. Laurent, which gave Guyane its Devil's Island reputation, ruined the wealthy whites. Disturbed only by spotty colonization schemes, by the middle of the eighteenth century the lack of adequate communication with France made Guyane a poor but self-sufficient colony. The small farmer, called Massagan, planted annatto and the wealthier planter, sugar cane and coffee.

In Martinique, a natural calamity befell the wealthy white Creoles on the morning of May 8, 1902. That day, the Mount Pelé volcano erupted and destroyed the city of Saint-Pierre and its inhabitants. St. Pierre had been the capital of the French West Indies and of Creoledom.

Besides the Haitian Revolution, the rise of the Second Republic in France was, perhaps, the hardest blow suffered by the wealthy white Creoles. Instituted in 1848, this government abolished slavery and gave the right of French citizenship, including universal male suffrage to the black population of Guadeloupe, Guyane, and Martinique. Although the wealthy whites did not lose their economic domination over these colonies upon emancipation, their remaining power was fraught with incertitude, and they lived in dread of retribution from the former enslaved Africans.

The people of color

At the other end of the French colonial society was the black community. It consisted of two main groups: the people of color and the blacks.

Born in the colonies, the person of color was the product of a white master and an enslaved African union and the marginal offspring born of Europe's mercantile adventure and of Africa's labor.

At the beginning of colonization, the sexual relationship of French men, who had ventured to Guadeloupe, Guyane, Martinique, and St. Domingue, with African slaves, was not in the legal or moral sense regarded as illicit. To the men who at first traveled alone, intercourse with women of other races was a necessity of milieu. The Spaniards, before the arrival of the French, had already crossbred extensively with Arawak and Carib women. According to contemporary accounts, "the Spaniards eagerness to take Indian women as concubines went to such extremes that it became all but impossible for an Indian male to find a wife, which contributed to the extermination of the tribal ethnic entities."[14] The Spaniards utilized the "Mestizo" to attack Mexico, "and later as the nucleus of loyal forces that Spain sought to maintain [in Mexico] for immediate action against any uprising of the dominated peoples."[15] The French, in turn, sought to do the same in their colonies with their mulatto offspring.

However, fifty years after the establishment of the French colonies in the West Indies, the metropolitan government, having concluded that the unabashed crossbreeding was a threat against its monopolies, made it illegal and prescribed in Article IX of the Code Noir punishments against intercourse between the free and the slave. It was thus that the *concubinage* of free and slave became statutorily criminal. When obeyed, it was, therefore, the women of color who had until the Code Noir been of their white father's status who became (until European women were introduced on a wide scale) wife and mistress to the Europeans. The men of color, who as auxiliaries to the Europeans, could not at that time compete for women of their own color, turned to African women. The unmarried free man who had children by a slave was compelled to marry her, to change her and their children's status to that of free.

The wealth of the planters attracted French women to the colonies who, unable to marry into a noble family at home, traveled to the West Indies to be wife to a waiting planter. Not only women who had aspired to marry into nobility traveled there, however. The majority were of the lower class who gambled on the scarcity of white women to strike it rich. The government also shipped women—from orphanages, for example—to the colonies.

Men who had no compunction at intercourse with women of other races recoiled when women of their own race arrived in the colonies. This phenomenon was not unique to the French West Indies. Records abound of racial prejudice following closely behind the introduction of white women in colonies. Sexual customs had their way in the development of race relations where Europeans settled in the tropics. However, the growth of racism toward the people of color does not date entirely to the arrival of French women, although Julien Raymond, in 1791, maintained the opposite view.[16] Then, too, European women looked upon women of color as rivals; however, in a slavocracy, they had little difficulty upholding their interests.

In addition to the wealthy whites' monopolization of colonial privileges now that they had no need for the people of color to bear either their children or protect them against the enslaved Africans, incoming Europeans, especially to the islands, vied for the property that the people of color had owned for generations.

However, the overwhelming factor in the evolution of discrimination toward the people of color lay in the slavocracy itself, which so clearly divided master and slave by race. Consequently, as the colonial enterprise developed fully, it became a matter of masters' prestige, status, honor, and wealth and, later, survival as a racial entity, not to incorporate the blood of African or enslaved person into one's patrimony—not to have any misalliances in one's heritage. For, no matter how far removed was the person of color from ancestral Africa; the tint always followed and would be passed on. "This obsession against marrying anyone who might have 'colored blood' is one reason a wealthy white Creole knows—or claims to know—the genealogical tree of every family; the name of the family thus becomes a guarantee of purity."[17] Julien Raymond wrote about an M. Guérin, churchwarden but husband of a woman of color, who in 1762 was stripped of his office after some months because the Port-au-Prince council had decreed that a white *mesalliés* could not enjoy such honor.[18] The new mores forbade only marriages between white men and women of color, not *concubinage*. Nevertheless, it is apparent through comments by Moreau de Saint-Mery and others that *concubinage* lessened considerably as more and more women from France entered the households of wealthy whites.

Of course, it would not have mattered if the people of color had not been a distinctive group. But how could they not have been? Shunned by the wealthy whites who had incorporated and, at the beginning, given them freedom, education, and economic viability, they were also mistrusted by their darker brethren in the slave's pit. The stigma which slavery had imprinted on the African was, in any event, a gulf that no one who had tasted freedom could cross. The people of color, thus, turned to metropolitan France for equality with the whites in the colonies.

The military and clergy were inviting professions to young men who aspired to ennoble themselves in French society.[19] Until 1815, the constant state of war with Great Britain had compelled France to maintain standing armies in its West Indian colonies. Opportunities were plentiful for careers in the colonial militia. Young men of color as well as free blacks filled many of its ranks, including officers.[20] The added advantage of having commanding officers from France, often in open conflict against the white Creoles, was another inducement. Besides the regular army, there were companies manned mostly by free blacks and people of color specializing in the capture of escaped slaves. Called the *marechaussé* (mounted constabulary), this detachment, which had its parent organization in France, carried out its duties ruthlessly and was greatly feared by the blacks. The fact that France could arm blacks is an indication of the extent of the acceptance of the slaveocratic order by all concerned. Men of color also served in regiments in France, including the King's regiment itself.[21] Their loyalty to France was never questioned. Since the late seventeenth century, blacks have served in all the wars involving France, including the American War of Independence.

The militia and the *marechaussé* were not the only labor niches filled by men of color. In the colonial towns, they had virtual monopolies over tailor shops and barbershops. Many were barrel makers, cabinetmakers and of other skilled professions. Some artisans traveled to France, to place themselves in apprenticeship to guild masters.[22] Upon their return to the colonies, they were assured of a lucrative trade.

At the upper echelon of this group were the owners of property and slaves. They were the descendants of the first generation of mulattoes who had inherited land from their (white) fathers. According to Julien Raymond, leader of the free men of color, who himself owned property and slaves in St. Domingue, "Their land were, more often than not, the colonies best and the most productive."[23] However, on the eve of the 1789 French Revolution, only a few of these choice properties were still owned by the people of color. Raymond, who took part in the revolution, complains: "these same lands are now in the possession of whites who have dispossessed the people of color."[24]

Before slavery was abolished, the people of color feared to lose their freedom and even to be put back in the slave pit.[25] Where there were loopholes such as having a Carib instead of an African ancestor to ascertain one's right to freedom, a number of wealthy people of color brought such attributes into their genealogy. The majority, however, began in the second half of the eighteenth century to marry into metropolitan society. They did so for two reasons: First, the dowry for marrying into French society included the guarantee of French rights to the person of color. By marrying a son or daughter from the mother country, one invested in France for insurance of liberty. Second, like the wealthy white Creoles, the people of color feared the dissolution of their group and loss of their wealth either through low birth rates or through further crossbreeding with blacks. In the second instance, the reality of enslavement was always a concern.

The union of women of color with a French man usually took place in the colony. The well-to-do woman of color's dowry included land and slaves. Raymond reports that in 1763 more than three hundred French men, including many noblemen, married women of color.[26] The wealthy people of color sent their sons to be educated in France, where, besides an education, they often acquired a French wife. The sine qua non during these centuries of slavery was, for the people of color, not to be necessarily considered white per se but rather to be guaranteed the rights of French citizens. At the same time, they were obsessed with putting greater distance between themselves and the degenerating institution of slavery. To this end, they looked to France for salvation.

The Blacks

In addition, there were the blacks. Overwhelming numerically in comparison to the people of color—in 1779 the ratio was thirty-five slaves to each person of color in St. Domingue; twenty-five to one in Martinique; and sixty-one to one in Guadeloupe.[27] Before the French Revolution, there were, also, a small number of manumitted blacks whom the colonial authorities counted among the free people of color in official documents. There were approximately 1,500 of them in St. Domingue in 1791[28] in contrast to 270,000 slaves. They filled the ranks of the militia and the constabulary—positions that made them exempt from the capitation (tax) and provided security from re-enslavement. Others hired themselves out in the towns as gardeners and laborers and a few peddled their knife sharpening trade from door to door. In the French colonies, the free blacks held a very marginal and insecure economic status. And, although their position was considered higher than the slaves', the free blacks could never truly speak of the "bliss" of freedom.

The slave was the substance upon which the colonies thrived. He was not only the labor for the prosperity of the colonial establishment, he was also the gravitational center from which all status, resentments and fears took shape in these colonies. On a typical plantation, there were three categories of slaves. The *Nègre à Talent,* as the French title implies was a slave skilled in a trade. He was, for example, useful in building and maintaining the planter's house. He was also knowledgeable in the extraction of sugar from the *Saccharum* cane and in rum distillation. Planters held this group of slaves in high esteem and gave them preferential treatment. A number of them traveled to France with their masters, a few taking residence there.[29]

In colonies that did not practice "breeding" to replenish their slave supply and where, like in St. Domingue, newly arrived slaves constantly replaced deceased ones, the skilled slave was the most creolized because he survived the longest and worked in closest proximity to the planter. The skilled slave also was responsible for introducing the newly arrived Africans to Christianity.

They called a new African *Nègre piece d'Inde* or *Nègre Guinin* or *Congo,* meaning one not born in the Caribbean. The Navy Department levied a head tax on these Africans. They predominated in St. Domingue because that colony was such a beehive of activity and production it required more new slaves. St. Domingue contributed more to France's coffers than the other colonies, and the French government considered it its empire's gem. It manufactured sugar at a rate that made it the wealthiest colony of its day, and the absentee owners and the maritime bourgeois spurred the planters to produce still more. The result was decimation in the ranks of the slaves there. Still, by 1789 there were three times as many slaves in St. Domingue as in Martinique and Guadeloupe. The fact that they had not yet been culturally neutralized was as critical as their number to the future of St. Domingue.

The third category was the *Nègre à Culture*. Unlike the *Nègre Piece d'Inde*, he was not born in Africa but in one of the colonies. A field hand, he was used in every facet of colonial agriculture. In Guyane, he also fished and hunted for a master.

The *Nègre Maron*—the Maroon—the fourth in this repertory was a free African in the colonies. His colonial status was that of the slave who had taken residence in the hills or woods where Europeans would not dwell. The majority of Maroons devised their existence around the fear of recapture by the constabulary; and to remain free, they used every stratagem conceivable.[30] Communities of Maroons evolved and thrived in Jamaica as well as in Dutch Guiana (Surinam), and Guyane. Today there is still a viable autonomous community of *Nègres des Bois,* Bush Negroes, in Guyane and Surinam. In Guyane, the tribes of Saramacca and Boni occupy the Inini interior.[31] More than two thousand strong, they are related genetically to West Coast Africans. The Saramacca "religion, folklore, tribal organization, family patterns, modes of agriculture, art forms, and linguistic structure seemed to combine elements from Ashanti, Dahomey Benin, and the Congo."[32] The French assimilated Guianese looks upon the *Nègre des Bois* as "primitive." The Maroons determination to escape enslavement and maintain their own culture since the seventeenth century is still symbolized in their name for town dwellers: *Bahkra chlaff,* white man's slave.

Some Maroon groups were not just content to maintain their freedom by hiding; they also took up arms against the Europeans to drive them from the colony, knowing that the Europeans would always be a threat to them. In the early part of the nineteenth century, for example, an army of Maroons attacked the town of Lamentin in Guadeloupe.[33] They were defeated and the survivors hanged. Nor was this the only report of action against the slave establishment in the colonies by organized groups of Maroons. Until the end of slavery, planters lived in fear of the constant threat that the Maroon represented. His successes made him a legendary figure that was believed to possess supernatural strength. As such, the Maroon "was well served by the men of his race who regarded him as the personification of freedom from slavery and a living threat against their masters."[34] The favorite weapon of the Maroon was poison. Believed, by the Europeans, to possess innate knowledge of various plants,[35] the Maroon used poison extensively against the planters' live properties: slaves, cattle, dogs, mules.[36] The rationale for their actions was, if ruined, the planters would leave. Undoubtedly some did. As slave revolts became more frequent in the seventeenth and eighteenth centuries, the authorities prescribed severe punishments against the Maroons. "The price of slavery," concludes Eric Williams, "for the [European] colonials was eternal colonialism."[37]

Whereas in Guadeloupe, Guyane, and Martinique there is in every township a statue of an unknown soldier "dead for France," across from the presidential palace on the Champs de Mars in Port-au-Prince, Haiti, stands the statue of an *Unknown Maroon,* broken chains in hand, blowing on a conch to rally the Maroons.

The statue of Le Maron Inconnu in front of the presidential palace in Port au Prince, Haiti. Martinique, Guadeloupe and Guyane display the statue of Victor Schoelcher freeing the slaves. Haiti exhibits the statue of the Unknown Maroon freeing himself.

Chapter Eight
The Colonies—Victory and Defeat

St. Domingue's victory

As the Estate General prepared to reopen in 1789, after more than a hundred and fifty years of silence, the people of Guadeloupe, Guyane, Martinique, and St. Domingue operated the slaveocratic machinery not perceiving an end to slavery.

The Creole planter believed that his master's prestige based upon symbols of race and wealth would safeguard his domination over the colonies forever. The people of color, the most educated class in the colonies, sought not the equality of all races that would, in fact, have made them more secure as a group, but for France's recognition of them as Frenchmen. The blacks, who unknowingly held the balance of power, were terrorized for fear they would rise to claim their freedom.

The Estate General provided the fissure through which the slaves poured out of the plantations. As the question of representation and equality turned into open warfare between the people of color and the wealthy white Creoles, a group of Maroons in St. Domingue led by François Bookman made plans on August 14, 1791, for a slave uprising.[1] As the two upper classes battled each other, the blacks, whom both agreed must remain in slavery, took control of events.

Julien Raymond, principal exponent of the people of color's drive for equality at the national convention, wrote a long discourse on the method needed to suppress the slave revolt in St. Domingue that he called "a counter-revolution." This is a key document for it reveals the people of color's views vis-à-vis the blacks with whom they would share the nation of Haiti ten years later. In his proclamation, Raymond urged the blacks to return to the plantation and, as significantly, trust in the "powerful and generous [French] nation."[2] Raymond judged that the slaves did not yet have the "necessary virtuous soul" to be free. He, therefore, asks these "lost men to wait in respectful silence for the laws that will regenerate [them]."[3] Raymond told the slaves who had used arson on a wide scale in their drive for freedom that the "first thing that the law demands in the state of liberty and sociability is the respect of people and property."[4] The first quality for slaves who had left the plantation was "love of work."[5] Raymond assured a people who had just freed themselves that his "advice" was assuredly right because "the French themselves practiced them."[6] The people of color, of whom Raymond was an unflagging representative, wanted equality with the whites. They also wanted their property intact and the slaves back in the pit. In addition, they wanted the destruction of the hegemony of the planters who, in turn, wanted them in slavery or dead. To achieve their goal and keep St. Domingue and Guadeloupe coveted by Spain and England in French hands, the people of color were, after Ogé's death, forced to join the blacks who had number on their side. In light of the British danger to St. Domingue, there was a clamor to free the slaves, arm them, and loosen them against the British. In France, newspapers like *Le Patriote François* advocated, in 1793, giving the slaves liberty and "cover the soil of the colonies with fighters."[7] The people of color were also fearful that with the help of Great Britain, the wealthy Creoles would succeed in the scheme of making St. Domingue independent from France. The wealthy Creoles would then be able not only to confiscate the people of color's property but also obliterate the gains achieved in the Estate General and National Convention. Raymond called on the whites to forego all disputes, all recriminations and "above all no independence; let us remain devoted to France."[8] The planters' attachment, however, was to their properties and privileges.

The decree of February 4, 1794, only recognized the fait accompli of the blacks' self-liberation and the fact that they had saved the colony for France. Events followed a similar course in Guadeloupe where the Creoles, who had called upon Great Britain in their struggle to maintain slavery, were also defeated. There, as in St. Domingue, black leaders had no thought of breaking away from France. As the eighteenth century dawned, however, it was inconceivable that the status post the revolution would ever again be implemented. In accordance with St. Domingue's reality on the ground, Toussaint L'Ouverture, a *Negre à Talent*, drafted a constitution, reflecting the new day. Julien Raymond was a member of the committee elected to frame this constitution.[9] In article one, the constitution reiterated that St. Domingue was part of the French empire, noting, however, that the colony should have laws reflecting its own peculiarities. Article three forbade slavery forever; "all men were born, lived and died free and French." Articles Four and Five used the language original to the Declaration of the Rights-of Man and the Citizen that had its genesis in the French Revolution. These articles spoke of virtue and talents in lieu of any other distinction in employment. Like the Code Noir, Article Six admitted only one religion in St. Domingue—Catholicism. Articles Fourteen to Eighteen bound the laborer to the land and reiterated the protectionist policies of l'Exclusif. The eighth section of the constitution dealt with the government of the colony. Article

Twenty-seven, has a governor heading the administration of the colony to "communicate directly with the metropolitan government for all that is related to the interest of the colony." In Article Twenty eight, "Citizen Toussaint L'Ouverture, Generalissimo of St. Domingue, in recognition of the important services rendered the colony at the most critical juncture of the revolution and with the wishes of a grateful population" was named Governor of St. Domingue for life. In Article Thirty, Toussaint L'Ouverture was further given the right to name his successor. Many Haitian presidents have cited these two articles to legitimize the aim of remaining in office for life. One successfully succeeded his father. Article Thirty-one underlined that L'Ouverture's successor would swear to remain devoted to the French government. In none of the seventy-seven articles of the Toussaint L'Ouverture constitution was there any indication of freedom from the French empire. On the contrary, in a period when the colony was cut off from France because of the conflict with England and was believed to have been abandoned by its metropole,[10] the constitution was a reiteration of Toussaint L'Ouverture's and St. Domingue's attachment to the principles of the French Revolution and to France.

Napoleon's expedition to St. Domingue and Guadeloupe was already in full preparation when Colonel Vincent presented L'Ouverture's constitution to First Consul Bonaparte for ratification.[11] Napoleon used the constitution as a pretext to reinstitute slavery in the colonies

The force majeure, however, was freedom, which for the blacks was the primary goal. The fact that the majority of the 300,000 had not yet been culturally vitiated, these Africans in the Indies were an irresistible force. St. Domingue indeed "would soon be Haiti, better described as an African land with a few French characteristics than as a French land with certain African qualities."[12]

After the war of independence, those Afro-Haitians did not evolve into a constituent part of a "nation class." They instead became the "masses," the subsistence peasant farmers, separated by a caste-like canyon from the three percent of the population[13] that comprised the elite. This elite was made of the people of color who had joined the war with a view toward dominating the new government by dint of their culture and education, as well as keeping their properties and becoming Haiti's new aristocrats. Their cultural outlook, as it had been before the war, was French. That perspective was magnified by the pariah status that Haiti was saddled with as the first colony to become a nation from a successful slave revolution in the slaveocratic Western Hemisphere. The people of color wanted the world to look upon them as people possessing the influence of French culture. As a result, for more than a century, they widened the gulf separating them from the Afro-Haitians and Africa.

Also part of the elite was the black illiterate military officers who had positioned themselves at the apex of Haitian society with the support of the army. These soldiers received small parcels of land that could only provide food crops. At the outset of independence, Haiti deprived itself of a great number of the confiscated large estates and, subsequently, the cash crops that would have sustained its economy. A standing army was, however, of vital necessity since the French did not abandon their plan for the re-conquest of Haiti until the Haitian government agreed in 1825 to pay an indemnification of 150 million francs, between fifteen and twenty billion in today's American dollars. The leaders of the Haitian war of independence also understood the pitfalls of their insularity, of being cut off from the rest of the Caribbean. They also understood the need to divert Bonaparte from St. Domingue, now Haiti. Along that line, Haiti vainly attempted in 1802 to help the people of color overthrow the colonial government in Martinique.

For the new Haitian nation, Jacques Dessalines who, unlike Toussaint L'Ouverture, was not imbued with the idea of allegiance to France drew a new constitution,[14] of which Articles Twelve and Fourteen were of primary importance. Article Twelve stated that: "No white person, whatever his nationality would set foot in this country as master or landowner or would in the future be permitted to acquire property here." Until the American occupation in 1915, this article remained inviolate. Article Fourteen postulated that all Haitians were of one family, and as such were to be known under the generic denomination of black. Dessalines' wish to see the nation united under one racial banner did not materialize until Article Twelve was eliminated by white occupiers in 1918.

The Haitian elite scorned the masses and Haiti's African culture. Then members of this privileged class grappled with each other for government spoils of which the presidency was the highest prize. The people of color who guarded the gate of the elite's culture, and the blacks in the upper echelon of the army succeeded each other to the presidency twenty-six times between 1804 and 1915. Only twice during that period did a Haitian president leave office at the completion of a constitutional term.

Guadeloupe's defeat

Slavery would not have been reinstated in Guadeloupe had Louis Delgres and his men realized the desperate condition of Napoleon's troops on the island. "For a period in the summer of 1802 the French generals did not see how they could possibly win. Their situation at that time appeared to be more precarious in Guadeloupe than in St. Domingue."[15] Despite being the highest-ranking officer in Guadeloupe, Magloire Pélage's eagerness to demonstrate his loyalty to the French government led him to have his troops disarm upon the arrival of Bonaparte's expeditionary unit, and the freed slaves rebelled and inflicted a number of casualties on the French forces. In addition, an epidemic of yellow fever ravaged the ranks of the French troops in 1802. However, in the end, Napoleon was successful. Delgres and his men committed suicide. Delgres's "desperate action in firing the mine tipped the balance of forces in favor of the French."[16] Magloire Pélage's unilateral disarmament gesture in 1802 also played a vital role in the French ability to re-impose slavery in Guadeloupe.

Chapter Nine
Abolition—The Role of Cyrille Charles Auguste Bissette and Armand Barbes

In the first half of the nineteenth century, blacks and men of color devoted themselves to lobbying the French government to abolish slavery. The Haitian victory in St. Domingue and the struggle in Guadeloupe had exacerbated planters' apprehensions everywhere in the hemisphere. However, the planters' concern did not preclude the opened rebellion against slavery in Guyane, Guadeloupe, and Martinique. It was clear, to blacks and people of color, especially in Guadeloupe, that freedom was indeed attainable. In the phrase of Alexis de Tocqueville, "the sufferings that are endured patiently, as being inevitable, become intolerable the moment it appears there might be an escape." Amelioration of the slaves' condition and the rights of the people of color "served to reveal more clearly what still remained oppressive and now all the more unbearable," as de Tocqueville might have added in this case.

This period marked a modification in the sociopolitical attitude of the people of color toward the blacks. Prior to the 1789 French Revolution, the people of color had one primary concern: equality with the planters. Excluded from this scheme were the slaves. However, in the aftermath of the struggles in the colonies, the people of color began to underscore the necessity of an alliance with the black slaves in order to unseat the wealthy Creoles. A drastic change took place in the racial perspective that the people of color had of themselves. It accounted in part for the abolitionist work undertaken by men such as Cyrille Charles Auguste Bissette.

In their struggle for equality with the wealthy Creoles, the people of color had endeavored, before the French Revolution, to repudiate their African ancestry. "Instead of rejecting the system, [they] denied their own identity."[1] However, their freedom was threatened as long as slavery remained extant. Napoleon's re-imposition of slavery put that fact into greater perspective. Consequently, the post-bellum colonies witnessed a perspective change in the men of color. In their abolitionist activities, they gave recognition to what they were. "Permit a great-grandson of a black slave woman ..."[2] Bissette said in an open letter. He also wrote of "his compatriots, black and mulatto in the colonies"[3] and of his "brothers' rights to freedom."[4] Along with this recognition, emerged a new set of racial idioms. The slaves were now called "people who were not free" and the people of color "belonged to the old class of color." "Mulatto" which had been derogatory until then became preferable to "man of color."

There is no statue of Cyrille Charles Auguste Bissette in the French colonies. Erecting a monument to a man of color freeing slaves, as France did to Victor Schoelcher, would have been against the basic tenets of colonialism. However, Bissette published a newspaper dedicated to the abolition of slavery, which "more than anything else paved the way for the act of emancipation in 1848."[5] *La Revue des Colonies*, The *Colonies' Journal*, was the spirit that mobilized the abolitionists against detractors and slave owners.

For possession of a pamphlet describing the situation of free people of color in the French West Indies,[6] Bissette and seven other men were first sentenced to be exiled in 1824. The affair illustrates the virulent fear and desperation of the planters during this period. To deter a repetition of the revolution in the colonies, the Creoles who saw threats everywhere, struck at the people of color and the growing population of free blacks at every rumor of plots. But exile was not enough. In France, Bissette, and people like him, would join with other abolitionist partisans to clamor against slavery. Consequently, an appellate court in Martinique sentenced Bissette and two others to hard labor for life and to be branded. In his cell in Bordeaux, Bissette achieved *cause celebre* status. His case was debated in the streets and with it the need for colonial reform in France's colonies, the abolition of the slave trade, and the recognition of Haiti's independence.[7] In France, the Cassation Court voided the ruling of the Martinican court and appointed the appellate court of Guadeloupe to review the Bissette case. His two friends received light sentences. The court finally sentenced Bissette to ten years in exile. The importance of this case lies in the manner it galvanized the abolitionist forces against not only slavery but also against the surviving planters of St. Domingue living in France, where they lobbied the French government against recognizing Haiti's independence.

The Bissette affair also brought out those laboring against the forces contesting the assimilation policy in the colonies. And it gave Bissette the added resolve to oppose the planters and their colonial lobby. *La Revue des Colonies*, which began monthly publication in Paris in 1834, never missed an opportunity to strike at Bissette's *bête noire,* the planters. He wrote on all sorts of subjects pertaining to the French colonies. In the issue of June 1835, for example, he published an article about a free black man, a Freemason in Guadeloupe, whom some of France's most prominent government officials had initiated into their lodge. In the fight for emancipation and assimilation, the rationalist French Freemasons played a major role in collaborating with both blacks and people of color, opening another venue for association between the two.

Bissette also wrote about the achievements of blacks and men of color in fields, which, in an 1823 pamphlet, he had denounced as being closed to them. In the *Revue des Colonies* of September 1834, he named four men of color who had completed their medical studies at the University of Paris: Messrs. Clavier of Martinique; Virgile of Guyane; Salesse of Mauritius, and Merlet of Haiti.[8] Throughout his writings, Bissette re-echoed the theme that members of his race could successfully participate in French social life. And, in his arguments for the immediate abolition of slavery, he pointed at multiple evidence that men of color and blacks had achieved eminence, to disprove the planters' contention that enslavement was the African's natural fate.

The action of the republican Armand Barbes from Guadeloupe matched Bissette's energetic pen. Also living in Paris, this man of color, after many seditious acts, such as an attempt to overthrow the king, designed to draw attention to the plight of the slaves and the people of color in the French colonies, was sentenced to the guillotine in 1830, for seizing city hall with twelve hundred men.[9] The people of Paris, together with Victor Hugo, appealed to King Louis-Philippe who commuted Barbes's sentence to life imprisonment at hard labor. But the most faithful defender of the cause of French republicanism, the ideals of the French Revolution and the Rights of Man, assimilation and emancipation in the colonies was the French working class. They saw in the slavocrats the reflection of the class the people of Paris had risen against in 1789. The French worker's republican struggle during Louis-Philippe's reign and later during Napoleon III's gave impetus to the liberal movements on behalf of the abolition of slavery.

The dichotomy of ideals and interests that had divided France and the planters since the eighteenth century benefited the civil rights crusade men of color such as Bissette and Barbes championed. While these men had relative freedom of movement in France, they could not have survived in the colonies. Nor could the collaboration they enjoyed with prominent activists against slavery—men such as the Corsican-born Protestant theologian, Agénor de Gasparin and lawyer politician, François-André Isambert—been possible. Neither would the planters have allowed them to cooperate with members of the romantic school and those of France's republican circles that made their effort on behalf of abolition successful.

It is not surprising that these men of color-abolitionists never ventured outside of France and French ideas and principles. Emancipation had to be accompanied by the rights of French citizenship and access to French society. Having vested assimilation with salvationary powers, their fervor toward it knew no bounds. In the end, the men of color, and later the children of the freed slaves, wagered their future on France's assimilationist tendency, betting at the window of their identity with what was in effect self-alienation. Their frame of reference never deviated from France's own.

The uproar that preceded the formal declaration of emancipation in February 1848 in Guadeloupe and Martinique came as a response to the overthrow of the monarchy and the proclamation of the republic. Such events provided opportunities the colonies took to promote abolition. One of the characteristics noted about these colonies' history is that major occurrences followed closely revolutions and other uprisings in France. Thus the colloquialism, "when France sneezes, the colonies catch cold."

The abolition struggle left the colonies out of breath. The former slaves and the people of color rested, seemingly with no other heights to climb. Commenting on the period following emancipation, Alfred Martineau and L. Ph. May said, "from 1848 to our day [1935] one can say that [Guadeloupe, Guyane and Martinique] have no more history. All the social claims are satisfied; there are no more struggles other than those of sometime contradictory interests created by a new economic regime, at the same time more liberal and more anarchic."[10]

The new citizens went to the polls to reward the men who, on their behalf, had militated against slavery. Bissette was one of those elected to the legislative assembly of Martinique. He had engaged in an acrid personal polemic against Victor Schoelcher, the French father of abolition, but the planters chose Bissette over Shoelcher and supported him in the 1849 election. The man, who twenty-five years earlier had been branded and condemned to the galleys, was welcomed home a hero. "The bay was covered with be flagged boats, the windows were full of flags, the crowd covered the Bertin Plaza; never had St. Pierre seen such enthusiastic ovation. Bissette was received in an indescribable explosion of frenzy."[11] Utter joy at being free marked the abolitionist's tour of the island the same year. However, his opportunistic alliance with the planters cost Bissette the support of the people of color. They turned their backs on him, ensuring that he would be overshadowed by his adversary Schoelcher to whom the French government erected countless statues in the colonies. With all the devices France could muster, Schoelcher—not Bissette—came to signify emancipation to the masses of former slaves. As France intended, the masses identified in Schoelcher the mother country that had abolished slavery. They saw through him France as the vector that, in spite of the recalcitrant planters, had brought them freedom.

However, to Napoleon III now in power, "assimilation was in complete contradiction with the principles of the imperial government. He considered the colonies conquered territories, and their population subjects not citizens."[12] The return of planter rule, the fear they would reestablish slavery, the working pass law, all became, for the first generation of former slaves, the new colonial reality. For the African indentured laborers who began arriving in 1852, existence was particularly harsh. The Creole blacks regarded them as unwelcome competition for the meager wages they both worked for at the plantations. Unable to strike at the planters, the Creole blacks struck at the indentured laborers. "African" became an epithet on the lips of the former slaves. They ostracized the newly arrived Africans; and looked on the newcomers as a reminder of Africa, which the creolization process had turned into a negative trait. Of this phenomenon, Frantz Fanon remarked that, in effect, "the colonized is elevated above his jungle status in proportion to this adoption of the mother country's cultural standards."[13] By rejecting the new Africans, they cast out their own background and psycho-surgically aligned themselves with the rulers. In the same vein of make-believe, they closed the economic gap between their own wretchedness and the dominating affluence of the white Creoles and the people of color. The African indentured laborer, in turn, looked to the metropolitan government for redress, identifying the former slaves as the oppressors, rather than the system that exploited him. As a result, the descendants of the indentured Africans are closely associated with the French government, which they serve in the police and the army and, it is rumored, as informers.

Assimilation within the French West Indies and Guyane

The reaction against Napoleon III's disallowance of colonial representation in Paris was evident by 1875. To Emile Alcindor, "the situation at that time in the Antilles had become similar to those of the French Departments. There was, from the legal point of view, no difference at least for the future."[14] However, by the turn of the century, there was a sense of foreboding apprehension that France's interest in Guyane, Guadeloupe, and Martinique was waning. Indeed, France had turned its attention almost exclusively toward Asia and Africa where it had acquired new possessions. Guyane, which had always suffered from colonial insecurity, was overwhelmed:

> when a rumor spread that someone in France had suggested that Guianese be deprived of their French citizenship and reduced to the level of subjects as in the new African colonies and deprived of their elected councils. People showed their consternation, protesting that they were not Africans, and hoped that their elected officials would act.[15]

In the French West Indies, dependency upon the mother country was at an equal level; and the people endeavored to show their worthiness for France's favors. Representatives to parliament were, for example, instructed to petition the government to give Guadeloupe, Guyane and Martinique the same "honor to die for France" as the decree of July 5, 1889, had given young Frenchmen. Two years before the start of World War I, obligatory military service was finally achieved in the colonies. They had the decisive trump card in the argument to solidify their amalgamation with France—they would die for the mother country. During World War II a great number of Martinique's young men including Frantz Fanon risked their lives crossing the Dominican Channel in small canoes to join de Gaulle's Free French forces. It is, however, in light of perceived interests that such show of fidelity is to be understood.

Until recently, it was unthinkable for the inhabitants to conceive themselves, even in a limited way, outside of France's protective umbrella. And although intergenerational mobility seldom occurs, members of the lowest class have, since emancipation, continued to put their expectation for a better life for their children into the hands of colonization.

Men of the lower class are the ones who have most often given their lives in France's wars, including the wars to retain the colonies. The mother country has rewarded them with departmentalization status, making them—theoretically—a part of France. During his visits, de Gaulle never failed to exclaim, "How French you are!" and to declare that, "all France remembers the glorious part you have played in her victories in the two World Wars."[16]

In response to permanent disappointments at their unfulfilled aspirations, the lower class of the French West Indies and Guyane are one with the Haitians, in the "belief in fatality [that]," according to Fanon, "removes all blame from the oppressor."[17] To them, "the cause of misfortunes and poverty is attributed to God: He is fate."[18] Besides impotent fatalism, the lower class has put the people of color on a pedestal. Confounding the achievements of this group with biological and phenotypical proximity to the rulers, a color tinge became a panacea that only illegitimacy could satisfy. The person of color, in accordance with tradition, seldom entered into a legal union with a black member of the lower class.

Assimilation as a policy and its affirmation by the people of the French West Indies and Guyane has so succeeded because of insularity and geographical smallness—especially the islands—but also because of the triumphant centuries of French colonization. Then, too, the French colonies were, for the most part, recipients of diverse African ethnic groups. In the Martinican parish of Carbet, for example, the baptism register is rich in recordings of the African nations from which the christened came. Information on two hundred and forty-six people reveal that from 1812 to 1831 thirty-nine were from Senegal-Mali; fifteen from Gambia; forty-seven from the Ivory Coast; one from Ghana; one from Togo; one from Dahomey. From Nigeria, there were eight Mokos and seventy-three Ibos (Igbos); two were from Gabon and forty-six from the Congo. Assimilation, which, in the colonial context, has for basic tenet the cultural neutralization of a conquered people, is more likely to succeed if diversity exists within the subjugated group. The rejection France suffered in Algeria, Indo-China, and St. Domingue-Haiti was due partly to the populations there being to a greater degree homogeneous; France did not experience this in the West Indies where there evolved a French-centered melting pot. Diversity was an asset to the colonization of the West Indies; homogeneity was a liability in other parts of the world.

Language and religion were also two formidable tools in the assimilationist's arsenal. With a creolized language which, in time, displaced that of Africa from individual memory, the Ibo person or the Mukongo assumed a creolized culture, which the priests reinforced by rewarding conformity with promises of heaven or by punishing disobedience with threats of perdition. In this newly-formed community, opprobrium was a particularly strong socializer. Backed against the wall of slaveocratic compliance, the black person developed guilt about himself, replacing his African culture with a bias toward French beliefs, behavior patterns, values and color. Aimé Césaire of Martinique describes the result of African cultural sterilization for the benefit of the mother country in these terms:

> And there are those who are not at all consoled at not being made in the likeness of God but in the likeness of the devil, those who believe that one is black as one is a second-class clerk anticipating better and with the possibility of rising above his state; those who beat the drum of surrender before themselves, those who live in their own pit; those who cloak themselves in proud pseudo-morphoses; those who say to Europe: "Look, I can bow and scrape like you, I can pay compliments; in short, I am not different from you; pay no attention to my black skin; it's the sun that has burned me.[19]

The drive for incorporation into the French nation reached another obstacle during France's German occupation. It was, beginning on August

3, 1940, forbidden to Jews, people of color, and blacks to be repatriated to the occupied zone. This decree provoked consternation and fear of lost of French citizenship in the colonies. Their representatives: Candace, Lagrosiliere, Calandou-Diouf, Satineau, and Monnerville dispatched a critical plea to Marshal Philippe Pétain, former French general and future chief of state of Vichy France, to express alarm at such a turn of event. This plea reveals the level of French assimilation that had taken place in Guadeloupe, Guyane, and Martinique. It read, in part, that:

> The French people of color do not know of any Armistice clause which distinguishes them from the French people of the white race ... the blacks and the people of color of our colonies ... will be deeply affected by the humiliation that the victor has imposed on them on French soil, for they, deep within themselves, worship the noble country which has given them dignity .... Educated and instructed by France, they have always endeavored to be worthy of her. In their heart they worship her, and in their minds one finds all the vibrations of the French soul ... The colonials molded by [France] are proud to be her adopted sons.[20]

Chapter Ten
Haiti in Literature from Independence to the American Occupation

An Overview

Writers of nineteenth century French West Indies obeyed the colonial aspiration to adapt and conform to French models. The environment conducive to the muses was exclusively French; there was no other influence. The conceptual perimeters were French.

Condescendingly referred to as "mimicry" or "decalcomania" by later generations, the literature of the French-speaking West Indies found its nineteenth century roots in the often close relationships between French writers and the aspiring colonial ones in France typically there as students.

Bertrand Russell observed that if we wish to see a period truly, we must not see it contrasted with our own, whether to its advantage or disadvantage: We must try to see it as it was to those who lived in it. Above all, we must remember that, in every epoch, most people are ordinary people, concerned with their daily bread rather than with the great themes of which historian treat.[1]

With Russell's reminder as guide, we note that the French-speaking Caribbean writers, their vista turned away from the reality at home, became attuned to minimizing, ignoring when not denying an African genesis or expressing anti-African biases. The literature of the French West Indies evolved from that vista.

The apprehension at furthering autonomy-oriented colonies impelled the French government to withhold educational institutions from them. For that reason, white Creoles and wealthy young men of color went to the mother country for their education. "In the Parisian colleges, it was French culture that they assimilated, the metaphors, the images born in the country of Ronsard and Du Bellay."[2] It followed then that he who "chose to respond to his passion to write, was condemned to look toward France."[3] There was no iconoclast among these writers.

The Haitian elite, unlike the people of color in the other French-speaking West Indian islands, bore the burden of ostracism from the West. To shed its "rebellious slave" status and "to show its willingness to belong to occidental culture"[4] the Haitians engaged in *sui generic* "Bovarism," a term used by Jules de Gaultier and Jean Price-Mars to denote a society in the grip of illusion, perceiving itself other than it really is.

Most of the nineteenth century was the Age of the Romantic Movement. That the precepts of this movement were attractive to equality-minded colonials is no coincidence. Romanticism was not only "above all things a movement of literary emancipation"[5] whose leading proponents were active in the dismantling of the old regime and classicism, but was also the advocate of "exotic causes" such as the recognition of Haiti's independence and the abolition of slavery.

It was in the immediacy of poetry that Romanticism found its most compatible outlet. Free of the restraints of systematic and planned verse, the young writer of the French-speaking West Indies could more easily abandon himself to the search for the French masters' poetic belles-lettres. To be sure, the *Meditation* of a Lamartine or the *Chanson* of an Alfred de Musset was psychologically tempting. It was, however, the brooding Victor Hugo who dominated the century "All those who wrote verses between 1830 and 1880 thought about him; tried to break free of his influence and despaired to exist close to this giant."[6] No poet—colonial or metropolitan—could match the French master. Indeed, Hugo had only substandard imitators.

The lyricism of the Romantics did not fit the compartmentalization of classicism. As such, the personal sensibility and imagination of Lamartine could only sound false and contrived when penned by an imitator. The fact that the parodist was a black or man of color doomed him to the criticisms and ridicule of later generations.

In the glow of independence, Haitian writers lent their talent, in the bombastic style of the French Revolution, to proclaim first, as did Antoine Dupré, that:

If, some day, on our shores

Tyrants dare come.

Let their fugitive hordes

Serve as fertilizers for our fields.[7]

Borrowed from the French national anthem written by Rouget de Lisle in 1792, this stanza is an example of the defiant patriotism—in the classicist style in vogue in Haiti immediately following the Haitian Revolution. The group that comprised the patriotic front in Haitian poetry adopted as their motto the slogan, "Sword and talent must have only one goal, to convey honor to the state."[8] A sterile and a self-serving slogan, the patriotic poets, soon, succumbed to the irresistible forces of the Lamartine *Meditation* published in 1820. They also gave in to their individual "Bovarism," especially following France's official recognition in 1825 of Haiti's independence. (Of particular note is the cost Haiti paid for freeing itself from France's tutelage. Haiti *never* recovered from the bankrupting price tag).

Although not typical of his age, Toussaint L'Ouverture's son Isaac (1785–1854) exemplified—as did his father—Haiti's attachment to France. In his *Hymn to France (Hymne à la France),* he wrote in 1828:

I am going to sing your glory, O France! O my Fatherland!

Noble sanctuary of the arts, cradle of industry.

I am going to sing your glory and looking into the future

Engrave in all hearts a pious remembrance.[9]

Isaac L'Ouverture's *Hymn* to the glory of France was much echoed by succeeding poets.[10]

With the advent of General Fabre Geffrard to the presidency, a renewal took place in Haiti following the dreary reign of Emperor Faustin Soulonque. Haiti's recognition by the United States and the Vatican further gave the lyricists additional options to express new sentiments through their "faith" in Hugo and Lamartine.

Lamartine and Hugo are two immortals.

They have my trust. I will pray at their altars.[11]

In France, Charles Baudelaire, with his *The Flowers of Evil* (*Les Fleurs du Mal),* published in 1857, added new insight into the poetic formula that radiated throughout the French-speaking world. Oswald Durand (1840–1906) initiated the newfound literary freedom with Haitian exoticism. Until then, Haitian writers satisfied the exotic requirement of Romanticism by following the lead of Victor Hugo who in the lines of the *Les Orientales* (1829), for example, contributed to the cause of the Greeks who had rebelled in 1821 against Turkish rule. The Haitian elite followed; rallied to the cause of the Greeks, and prepared to send troops to save the birthplace of European culture, as well as help maintain the right of all people to self-determination.[12] The elite later turned to Africa, to sympathize, in alexandrines verse, with the Afrikaners, proclaiming that

An enraged nation vows its hate to the British

And its love to the gallant Boers.[13]

In his poem, "Idalina," a Haitian woman inspires Durand as Hugo was stirred by "Sara la Baigneuse." Side-by-side these two poems exemplify the Paris—Port-au-Prince connection. In the same breath, Oswald Durand mourns,

Why then am I a Negro?

Oh, why then am I black [14]

His taste for the exotic as well as a remarkably talented pen equaled that of the poets of the new Parnassianist and, later, the Symbolist schools, without losing faith for a moment in Hugo and Lamartine. In these verses about a Voodoo ceremony, Durand demonstrates the "perfection of form" and the "art for art's sake" traits of the Parnassians:

In the gloomy distance spread with white huts,

The drum bellows the mysterious chant

Of the magical voodoo, with divine raptures

Where a he-goat is being sacrificed,

Where vases are being smashed,

Intoxicating the fathers who beat impetuously

The drum bellowing the mysterious chant

In the gloomy distance spread with white huts.[15]

This assiduous and energetic poet also wrote of love. That of a man of color—himself—for a French woman:

At age twenty, I liked Elise. She was white and frail.

I, the son of the sun, alas, too brown for her;

I did not receive a glance from her astonished eyes!

...The son of the black man frightened the white man's daughter.[16]

In this stanza, Aimé Césaire's later admonition about the belief that one is black as one is a second-class clerk is evident when Durand interjects: "Alas, too brown for her."

The political situation in Haiti during the nineteenth and early twentieth century, imperceptibly at first, began to imprint its mark on the literature. As the ruling elite of color and the army fought each other for supremacy over the country, the men of letters found inspiration in the betrayal of the Haitian Revolution. An example was a stanza by Isnardien Vieux in 1896:

From our valiant forebears we sell the heritage.

Like the fratricidal assault of battles,

Mourning each day under the shore's wind,

Of our peaceful seas, makes the waves sob.[17]

Others, such as Tertullien Guilband, simply despaired:

I do not understand them, these long sunless days,

These long perfumeless evenings. The cold and gray dusk

Whose clouded sky, throws to the bottom of my heart,

Its dismal reflection. I feel my soul taken over

By a deadly anguish.[18]

But there was also Massillon Coicou (1867–1908) to write these prophetic verses in 1892:

Ah! If you forget that your sharp blows fall

only on you. You will remember them

When, one day, Jonathan, John or Jack, or anyone else

Come knocking at your door.[19]

In these verses, Coicou echoed the country's despair and sense of futility, as well as the leaders' inability to resolve their fratricidal power struggles. But, more importantly, Coicou gave warning that the country's weaknesses were leaving the door open to foreign intervention that did in fact take place twenty-three years later.

In *The Ten Black Men (Les Dix Hommes Noirs)*, published in 1901, Etzer Vilaire (1872–1951) gives testimony to Haiti's internal misfortunes at the end of the century. It was a time when people of the urban poor chose suicide over wretchedness,[20] as well as a time when the ruling elite of color and their darker counterpart blamed each other for the condition in which the country had sunk. In this long poem in rhyming couplets, Vilaire proposes to voice the disillusion of the elite's youths since 1804,[21] noting the elite's failure to find in Haitian life anything conducive to their intelligence or talent. "A moral sickness rages at home with frightening acuteness and this poem is its bitter fruit."[22] It is also a wish for death to cleanse and, perhaps, to renew:

The star in order to shine waits for the sky to darken.

Sadden, the shadow cries, dark, and its dew

Gives birth to pearls on the tired ground:

As a result, the soul cracks up and blossoms off its ills.[23]

The Ten Black Men is also directed against the "crude" military class that the "enlightened" people of color despise:

They had met in the army. Piled up

On the stinking pallets of the terrible barracks;

Walking their pale profiles into taverns.

They were wearing themselves out from the idleness and

the boredom of peace.

Then they left that crude phalanx

Keeping only their sad uniforms.[24]

The army was indeed a rabble with bad intentions. Maintained to keep the classes in their respective places, government leaders used the soldiers to repress oppositions at all levels of Haitian society. To a man of color such as Vilaire, the black upper echelon of the army in power at the time was the cause of Haitian woes. "The truth is that Heads of State are recruited most often among members of the ignorant and brutal army. Jealous of their authority, they have left little initiative in the enlightened men [of color] whom they condescendingly hire, seeing with a bad eye the necessity of asking them for advice, and instinctively distrusting them."[25]

In 1922 Vilaire was appointed to a judgeship by a president from the "enlightened" class.

The conflict (for autocratic) power between blacks represented by the nationalist party and people of color by the liberals was resolved with coups d'état and repression that often led to civil war. At sixteen, Vilaire witnessed the 1887 rebellion of the liberals against President Lysius Salomon and the ensuing civil war that lasted until the election of Florvis Hyppolite ten months later. One of "*The Ten Black Men*," three times, had conspired to overthrow the government:

Three times I conspired against a tyrannical chief ....

I could have eased myself smoothly into power,

If I had managed to bend a little my inflexible knees.[26]

Unlike a number of critics of Haitian writing who, as early as 1875, demanded less imitation of foreigners, and a literature more reflective of Haiti's realities, Vilaire was representative of the "enlightened" group of writers who thought it an "error to require that Haitian poetry limit itself to the description of [their] marvelous tropics."[27] His dream was to initiate "a French literary elite."[28]

Writers less imbued with France's literary prestige and more concerned with the elite's race, its cultural, economic and political annihilation were circumventing that dream. Vilaire was embittered that his compatriots were deviating from his ideal in their seemingly thoughtless desire to improvise an autonomous literature.

Frederic Marcelin is typical of the group of writers who, at the turn of the century, began, in prose, to describe the reality of Haitian life, including the peasantry's. His *Themistocle Epaminondas-Labastere* published in Paris in 1901, was greatly criticized for giving so many details about Haiti.[29] Using satire and humor, *Themistocle* brought to light the mores of Port au Prince's businessmen and politicians. The novel also gave life to a number of unsavory characters in a realistic Haitian setting.

Justin Lhérisson published two novels on Haitian life using the humorous approach. In 1905 *The Familiar Family (La Famille des Pitite-Caille),* and, a year later, *Zoune at her Godmother's* (*Zoune Chez sa Ninnaine*). Vilaire' s "The Ten Black Men," Marcelin's *Themistocle*, Lherisson's and other writers' works such as Fernand Hibbert's and Antoine Innocent's are drenched in lassitude and impotent inability to change Haiti's course toward disaster. These sentiments permeate in the guise of suicide or satire.

Even before 1915, Haitians' literary production at home and abroad was extensive. It seems that every man from the ruling class was struck at one time or another by the need to write.[30] In verse and prose, the cultured class found a sort of sedative to deal with the approaching debacle at home and perhaps to breach the gulf created to keep the masses at bay. The gulf was a strangling rope, which the army pulled ever so tightly.

As the elite lost its footing, its members clung to the memory of the victories that had led to independence. This was particularly true before France recognized Haiti in 1825 and again during the "humiliating years," which as early as 1891, foredoomed Haiti to foreign occupation. That year, the United States requisitioned the harbor of Mole St. Nicholas in the northwest peninsula region from the Haitian government. However, due in great part to the influence of Frederick Douglass, appointed Haiti's United States Minister in 1888, the project was later abandoned. In July 1899, to collect debts, the French bank in Haiti requested the receivership of the country's customhouse. By August, it was clear that Haitian and foreign creditors were withholding loans to the government in order to drive the country into insolvency, calculating that the Americans would then have to intervene. Three years earlier, the German government—a gunboat in the Port au Prince Harbor—had demanded and received in four hours the payment of a twenty thousand dollar indemnity to a German citizen whom a Haitian court had tried for bankruptcy. For good measure, it ordered a twenty-one gun salute to its flag. By 1900 the elite had come to believe that Haiti's independence, to the shame of past glories, was lost.

Despite Europe's censure against the St. Domingue rebellion, many Haitians felt that, because Haiti was the first black nation to gain its freedom in the new world, "it had," in the words of former Minister for Foreign Affairs, Antenor Firmin, "a duty to serve in the rehabilitation of Africa."[31] Frederick Douglass stated that "we should not forget that the freedom that you and I enjoy today, that the freedom that has come to the colored race the world over is largely due to the brave stand taken by the black man in the world."[32] And in 1900, Hannibal Price's *The Rehabilitation of the Black Race by the Republic of Haiti* was posthumously published in Port au Prince.

Within the Haitian elite consciousness of race was not lacking. Even an Etzer Vilaire could state overtly—if only—that he was a descendant of the black race of which he was proud to belong.[33] It was the cultural mold that had been lost. Vilaire, for example, perceived himself undeniably a descendant of the black race but alienated from Africa's culture, which he had thwarted in favor of French aestheticism. There lay the perennial conflict between the elite of color and the rest of Haitian society, between the foreign culture espoused by the former and the culture of Africa, the masses' own.

Critics formulate Haiti's cultural dilemma in racial terminologies. The French abolitionist Victor Schoelcher, for example, proposed, "the day mulattoes and especially the women call themselves Negroes we will see a distinction contrary to the laws of fraternity disappear. We are not dissimulating this fact, for that is the virus, which at this hour is decimating the population of Haiti and driving it to ruin."[34] Schoelcher mistakenly thought that "skin color differentiation was the unique cause of the anarchy devastating the Haitian Republic."[35] Then, too, he and the people of color were firm believers in reliance on French culture to take the black peoples in France's colonies to "the path of civilization" and equality. In the same breath with his trust in French culture, Schoelcher held that "any man having African blood in the vein could never do enough to rehabilitate the Negro name which slavery had degraded; it is for him a filial duty."[36]

On July 28, 1915, a detachment of Marines from the United States occupied the capital of the Republic of Haiti and put the ruling elite on the path to self-analysis and discovery of its Haitian roots.

Chapter Eleven
The Literature of the French West Indies and French Guiana from Emancipation to Publication of Batouala

Writers in the nineteenth century French West Indies were much less prolific than the Haitians during the same period. Although their work was of the same *bovaristic,* escapist tendency, the French West Indians felt less compelled to demonstrate how culturally western they were. Whereas the Haitian writer sought, however unsuccessfully, to convince Europe that African descendants were able to adopt European culture and, therefore, had a right to remain independent, the primary goal of the French West Indian writer was to achieve complete amalgamation of his colony into the mother country. The blacks and people of color of Guadeloupe, Guyane, and Martinique continued to perceive their best interests to lie in assimilation not in independence. To them, freedom meant escape from Africa and slavery and realization of socio-political incorporation into France. Consequently, the French West Indian writer aspired that his work would be an extension—a regionalization—of France's own. They were not only adherents but also exponents of the Romantic School. Many such as Privat d'Anglemont of Guadeloupe were themselves pioneers and leaders of the movement. However, these early Romanticists found it more profitable to their talents, and to their purse, to remain in France where most of them had gone to study.

In the colonies there was, in 1872, the Social Romanticist from Guadeloupe, Eugene Agricole. In the following poem, he says "farewell" to his native Basse-Terre and "greetings" to Martinique:

I must leave you Oh my dear Basse-Terre

And live far away from you

Where I have always found true friendship

A fire so sweet to me.

Greetings, three times greetings, Oh beautiful Martinique,

Laborious child of the Gulf of Mexico. Pleasant dwelling!

The breath of misfortune respects your crown,

And the treasures the heavens in its goodness gives you,

Increase each day.[1]

These stanzas characterize Romanticist versification with the new "Charm of the West Indies" theme. It portends the school of French West Indian "exoticism" later named "Regionalism" in keeping with the integrationist goal of the colonies. In the second stanza, the poet recalls the French intervention in Mexico where, in 1862, France sent a contingent from Martinique to "labor in the Gulf of Mexico." The stanza also denotes contentment with conditions in Martinique in 1872 when "the breath of misfortune respected [the colony's] crown."

Victor Duquesnay of Martinique brought French West Indian poetry closer to Regionalism with such works as "The Women of Martinique," ("Les Martiniquaises"). In this work, the author's native village of Marin and its people have replaced themes with local color:

Clear voice of a woman with peasant charms;

The overseer follows from a distance at his horse's pace.

Across the deserted fields,

Dawn turns on its summer shine on the sugar cane leaves.[2]

These verses romantistically illustrate the return of a peasant woman from a sugar cane field. The motif of peasants at dusk was much favored by the French Romanticists, particularly Victor Hugo. The stanza shows how completely disconnected from the existence of the West Indian laborer its author was.

Fernand Thaly, also of Martinique, provided excellent examples of regionalism with such poems as "The Bewitching City," ("La Ville Ensorcelante"):

Prodigious people! Under the swinging madras,

These girls of amber and gold, these women of red wood,

From the old Caribe blood ultimate reminder;

These collars, these turbans, these garbs whence having come,

These sphinx faces of an unknown race,

A people of once upon a time, who cannot come back![3]

In these verses, the poet recalls the old city of St. Pierre. Following the "catastrophe of 1902" when the Mt. Pelee eruption destroyed the city; afterward, St. Pierre was perceived as a mythical city. Everything there was said to have been superior and so on. Thaly in turn speaks of that city's "Prodigious people...of an unknown race created only once, who cannot come back."

Marcel Achard perfected the regionalist's style:

Here comes the evening on the thousand-flower island.

Silence dwells in the ravines' green furrow

And the sea birds fly back to the salt marshes;

Dusk has preceded the deep darkness.[4]

By means of "the thousand flower island" and "the marshes" metaphors, the poet indicates it is of Martinique, the flower island, he is speaking. Noticeable is the carefree tone with the theme depicting the "islands," as paradise on earth.

The Haitian writers' preoccupations were absent from the works of these colonial Regionalists. In their verses, the colonies are free of strife and misfortune; in this Eden, there is no hunger, no exploitation, and no racism. Their intention was, first, to lyricize in Romanticist verse, and later in Parnassian or Symbolist fashion, the beauty of their French region, nothing else.

Antoine de Gentile was another of the regionalists. In the following verses, he lightheartedly described a town's Sunday fiesta:

It is Sunday, the town has taken on a festive air.

The palm trees have offered their top leaves

To build roofs for the huts

Where swinging their hips to the rhythm of their footsteps

Mulatto women, laughing confidently,

Put syrups in your almond milk.

And the West Indian punch, perfumed with lemon,

Makes the heart sing and the forehead perspire.[5]

This stanza could be used on any travel agency's publicity poster specializing in white beaches and swaying palm trees. The poet has succeeded in conveying the feeling of peacefulness in an exotic setting. Here superficiality is given full poetic prominence at the expense of colonial realism.

Daniel Thaly was known as the "Prince of Poets" of the French Antilles following the publication of his *Lucioles and Cantharides* in 1900. Born in Dominica in 1879 of a Dominican mother and a Martiniquan father from St. Pierre, he began his studies at the old high school there; went on to medical school in Toulouse, where he first set in verse his recollections of the West Indies and his love of France. *In The Antilles* is an example of Thaly's dual sympathies for Toulouse and the West Indies:

If Toulouse charms me, oh my beautiful Antilles,

It's because its light like yours is Spanish.

Because the soft beauty of its spirited girls

Is sister to the happy indolence of the Creoles.[6]

Daniel Thaly, like his brother Fernand, found inspiration in the regionalists' theme of uncompromised "West Indian beauty and charm." Until his death in 1950, the "Prince of Poets" wrote nine books of poetry and many other poems published in several literary reviews in Martinique. Thaly, throughout his works, remained true to the regionalist's theme of an imaginary Antilles. He owed his title of "Prince of Poets" of the French West Indies to his mastery of the Parnassian poetic techniques.

The Parnassian School was founded as a reaction against the Romanticists' lyricism and sentimentality. Its leader was Lecomte de Lisle, a Creole from Reunion, a French island colony in the Indian Ocean, residing in France. The Parnassian poets strove for impersonality, detachment and exactitude in their descriptions of the exotic. In that they succeeded; their verses are precise in form, their descriptions almost scientific and empty of feelings. The French West Indian writers of the period followed these precepts, adding local color to the Parnassians' art for art's sake to found their own regionalism.

Under the pen of the Regionalists, they never speak of Africa from the point of view of writers from a colony peopled by former slaves. It was—when done at all —written as if the poet was himself a colonizer. They looked on French policies toward Africa as "our" policies." The following lines from *Prayer for Mankind* by Fernand Thaly demonstrate this phenomenon:

Let's look at the men marching.

At these sweating blacks carrying us, singing.

And if we are joyful, if we are happy

To go meet the elephant, the unicorn or the buffalo,

Let's say to ourselves that it would somehow be foolish,

A little bit simple and childish, a little bit sad and petty,

To possess Africa, and ignore the African.[7]

René Maran, baptized in Martinique of Guianese parents, grew up in France. Unlike his countryman, Felix Eboué, he was also a man of letters. Before his contact with Africa, Maran, one of the rare literary personalities from Guyane at that time, also participated in the regionalist's movement as this stanza from his poem *Tropiques* demonstrates:

Delta of the Maranon, mouths of the Orénoque,

Llanos, plantations, pieces of immensity

Where they pick while singing bunch by bunch

The tobacco summer has dried.[8]

These lines are the exceptional ones in which a writer describes areas of Guyane almost in idyllic terms.

These writers, in addition to the many others, who, like them, wrote under the banner of Romanticism or of Parnassianism, etc., belonged to the colonial strata of either wealthy Creole or people of color. The latter group had been in the best position to benefit from the elitist system of education instituted in the French West Indies and later in Guyane following the abolition of slavery. Consequently, for about a century, their works and those of a very small number of Creoles dominated the literary scene. The most famous Creole was Saint-John Perse, born in Guadeloupe in 1887, winner of the 1960 Nobel Prize for Literature.

Through their racial and social perspectives, they portrayed the former slaves who had become their servants, field hands, gardeners, etc., as exotic pieces in their poetic games. In turn, the rare black man who achieved prominence also had a game. Although different from the one played by the people of color, it also constrained him to a form of art for its own sake. He named it stoicism. The best-known players were the

French-speaking Guianese Felix Eboué (1884–1944, the governor of French Equatorial Africa, 1940–1944) whose motto was "play the game without changing the rules,"[9] and René Maran (1887–1960, another French Equatorial Africa colonial administrator).

> Eboué and Maran decided they were stoics ... These ideas clearly comforted Eboué at various troubled times. In conversations and correspondence he often cited a phrase from a stoic or pythagoreans [Eboué was also a Mason] to help himself or René Maran bear a disappointment or a humiliating experience ... Stoic philosophy did provide an ethical system which could appeal to people born in the old colonies who participated in the culture and politics of the empire.[10]

They adopted stoicism to sustain them in the face of racism in France and at the Colonial Office, which Eboué and Maran had both joined at the turn of the century.

Impassiveness toward humiliation and rationalization of shameful events in one's relations with the mother country were methods many blacks used to overcome disappointments. Fanon, the psychiatrist, explained the phenomenon in these terms: "While in Europe irony [which] is a mechanism of defense against neurosis protected against existential arguments."[11] Insulated from reality by irony or stoicism or both, Eboué found no contradiction in serving France in French Equatorial Africa as Governor from 1940 to 1944. Irony kept him apart from the Africans of the vast domain he governed, as well as from the black consciousness movements coming on line at that time, while his stoical, calm appearance in the face of insults to his race, and past promotion failures made him prone to respiratory illnesses.[12]

The regionalist poets[13] and men such as Eboué were not individuals shackled to the French poetic denomination or philosophy of the day. They were colonials who had chosen the manner they thought best to participate in the culture and politics of the empire. In the literary sphere, there were already, before the turn of the century, the schools of subjective symbolism, realism, naturalism, and the school of political and ideological commentators. In French philosophy, nationalism, Gobinism, and violence were the tendencies when Eboué chose stoicism. For the French West Indian writers of that time to have chosen a discontentment theme or for Eboué to have become a Guianese nationalist would have been against the advantages they perceived French assimilation to hold for both the people of color and the small black elite of the French colonies in the Caribbean. To that end, these men propelled Guadeloupe, Martinique, and Guyane into a higher stage of colonization, "autocolonization."[14] This doctrine led the colonials to be unnecessarily conservative, i.e., more than the demands from metropolitan France then required them to be, for fear of offending the mother country. An example of this phenomenon was the reaction to the publication, in 1921, of *Batouala* by René Maran. Whereas in France's literary circles they praised and awarded the book the distinguished *Prix Goncourt*, in assimilationist circles in the colonies it was virulently denounced for its anti-colonial sentiments.[15]

Chapter Twelve
The New Trend Batouala and the Color Line

In 1910 René Maran went to Oubangui-Chari, present day Central African Republic, as a French colonial administrator. For ten years, he lived among the people of that territory, the Bendas; witnessed their daily lives, and was appalled at what he saw. *Batouala* is the tale of the Mokoundji, the Chief, by that name. It is also the story of the people of Oubangui forced to labor under the *Code de l'Indigénat*, France's Black Code for its African colonies. In the story, Maran depicts the lives of the Bendas, and he uses the foreword to *Batouala* to denounce in explicit terms *l'Indigénat* and French colonial rule in Africa.

We meet the Benda's Mokoundji, Batouala, in media res. He is a chief. He has nine wives, but the one he prizes most seeks the arms of a younger man. Batouala, jealously, attempts to chase his rival away but is killed in the effort.

Penury is the upshot of France's colonial rule where Batouala and his people live. The authorities force the people to work in the rubber plantations in order to pay the taxes necessary to support the colonial administration of which Eboué was also a part from 1910 to1944. Coupled with the payment of taxes, there is suppression of religious practices and general disruption of the Benda's way of life. The Makoundji depicts what life for the Bendas has become under French rule in these terms:

> Not satisfied to suppress our customs, they wish to impose their own on us: 'You must no longer play patara for money!' We may no longer get drunk. Our dances and songs keep them awake. They allow it if we pay. 'Pay, pay; it's always pay.' Government coffers are insatiable.
>
> But then everybody knows that from the first day of the dry season to the last day of the wet season our work only pays the taxes when it does not also line the commander's pockets.
>
> We are taxable flesh! We are only beasts of burden! No, not even beasts! Dogs! Well, no, they feed their dogs, and they care for their horses. But we, we are less than these. We are the basest of the base. They are killing us off, by degrees.[1]

According to Maran, *Batouala* is entirely objective:

> It has taken me six years to write down what I heard and what I saw out there. In those six years, I have not yielded once to the temptation to put in one word of my own. I have preserved all objective attitudes so conscientiously that all reflections have been suppressed which could possibly be attributed to me. It does not even attempt an explanation: it is a testimony. It does not criticize; it registers. I could not do otherwise. On moonlight nights, from my long chair on the veranda, I listened to these poor folks talk. Their jokes were proof of resignation. They suffered, and laughed at suffering.[2]

Maran then expresses his indignation at the famine and blatant exploitation that he witnessed and took part in:

> I understand. What does it matter to Sirius if ten, or even a hundred, natives, in a day's distress, seek nourishment in undigested grains of maize and meal from horse dung—dung from the horses of their pretended benefactors?
>
> Montesquieu was right when he wrote in words whose cold irony vibrates with deep indignation: 'They are black from head to foot. Their nose is so flattened, it is impossible to pity them.'
>
> After all, if they perish of hunger by the thousands like flies, it is because their land is being 'worked.' Let those die who cannot adapt themselves to civilization.[3]

Since he was part of the French colonial administration in French Equatorial Africa, it is fair to say that in criticizing France's policies there, he was criticizing himself. He and France were in it together. With his epoch-making novel,[4] Maran did not wish to put distance between himself and France's policies in Africa. As he says, "my book is not a polemic. It comes by chance, at its appointed time."[5] Had he done so, he surely would have also written of France's policies in Guyane his homeland, which was "suffering" as badly as Oubangui-Chari. Maran, rather, like Fernand Thaly, also regarded France's colonial policies as "our" policies. *Batouala* was, therefore, written neither from a black man's sense of disquietude at the plight of Africans, nor as an act of rebellion against France and its colonial practices. In writing *Batouala,* Maran was responding to his outrage that colonial officers were disregarding France's stated "rights of man"[6] by recruiting Bandas for forced labor to pay their taxes. For assistance, Maran invoked France's unique unwritten rule of immunity for men of letters.[7] It was, therefore, to his fellow writers that he appealed. "O my brother writers of France, the honor of my country to which I owe everything. Writers for all parties, whenever it is a case of fighting for a just and noble idea, I call on you, for I have faith in your generosity."[8]

But Maran was judged by his colleagues in the colonial administration, in conservative circles in France, the West Indies and Guyane not as a Frenchman who like many others was denouncing colonial policies in Equatorial Africa, but as an ingrate. Had *Batouala* been the work of a white French author, Maran's life would not have been threatened nor his career compromised.[9]

Maran and *Batouala*, however, had their defenders. In Parliament, the two Guadeloupean representatives, Candace and Boisneuf, rose to speak in Maran's favour against charges of treason.[10] They were of the group, together with Eboué and others, who argued that Maran's Prix Goncourt was proof that a black Frenchman was equal to a white. This fact, they believed, would enhance further the assimilation of the French West Indies and Guyane into France.

And there were others who because he was black adopted Maran—notwithstanding his claim that he had written *Batouala* as any person of conscience would have done—as the first black from the French West Indies and Guyane to speak out against the evil of French colonial rule anywhere. With René Maran's *Batouala*, therefore, an accusatory landmark against colonialism was recorded in the literature of the French Caribbean Region.

Two years following *Batouala*, *The Color Line, Question de Couleur*, by Oruno Lara of Guadeloupe was published. Still written in the regionalist style, Lara's novel has the distinction of being the first where a man of color asserts explicitly that he is, indeed, what he is. Self-acceptance occurs while in France

I have white parents and I am not a Negro.

I have Negro parents and I am not white.

We are people of color

No, dear friends, we are Negroes.

You, not me.

You, like me!

Me? I will never say that I am a Negro![11]

The change in one's attitude in the face of racism in the Mother Country, from the stoic-ironic impassiveness to the defense of one's race, is also evident in Lara's novel. The protagonist has been the target of racism; he describes his reaction.

> More reasons, from now on, to throw out one's chest and to show off bravely! Yes! The best thing is to face squarely that idiotic color prejudice. It isn't a question of lowering one's head; of declaring oneself half-white, while cowardly turning one's back to the insults. And for what anyway? ... Better show oneself for what one is; say that one is black because one is and asserts the word 'black.'[12]

No longer on the level of irony, the man accepts his identity in others' attitude toward him.

Unlike *Batouala*, *The Color Line*, was not widely read.[13] "The colonial system," wrote Léon Damas, "did not permit regular contacts, from metropolitan France to colonies, or from colony to colony."[14] Lara's novel, however, achieved a breakthrough.

Lilyan Kesteloot affirmed that: "before *Legitime Defense* [published nine years after Lara's novel] there was effectively no original [committed] literature in the French West Indies." *The Color Line*, in comparison to other works of the period, in fact, had taken a bold step in lifting the taboo from the subject of one's origin. Nevertheless, it was left to writers a decade later fully to give recognition to Africa as the major force in their culture.

Chapter Thirteen
Coming to Terms with Africa—Haitian Nationalism

The Americans in Haiti

Haiti had become synonymous with instability. In the capital, the masses had lynched the president, Guillaume Sam, who had taken refuge in the French Embassy; and the Germans, who had economic interests there, had turned Haiti into a geo-strategic annoyance for the United States. Had a World War, in which Berlin held center stage, not been waging on, Washington would have continued to take notice of Haiti from an angle that did not include the Marines.

The presence of white occupational forces on their soil overwhelmed the Haitians. The belief that an attempt to re-establish slavery was under way provoked an uprising among peasants in the north. Called Cacos, the revolutionary peasants of Haiti's northern region were by August of 1915 routed by a detachment of Marines. The elite that had welcomed the American occupation they believed would uplift the country from the chaos it was experiencing began to have doubts as foreign rule made its reality felt. The Americans in charge of the various Haitian departments during the occupation were military men who showed little respect toward the traditional position of the elite. Neither the elite's education nor its display of French culture impressed them. They perceived the people of color differently than did the French. Whereas the latter considered the people of color to be closer to themselves culturally, Americans made little distinction between blacks. Although they chose men of color and not blacks (an example was the choice of Philippe Dartiguenave over Rosalvo Bobo for president in 1915) to assist in administering Haiti, the people of color, in spite of their European culture, were racially black. The Americans turned on full blast against Haiti the prejudice and racism to which African Americans were accustomed. The fact that these American military men were perceived as coarse and boorish added to the elite's pique. H. P. Davis speaking on the relations between the elite and the occupiers said:

> Many Haitians of the upper class have been educated in France, ... they respond at once to courteous treatment and are equally quick to resent condescension and the feeling of racial superior-

ity which many Americans in Haiti made little or no attempt to conceal. This resentment was particularly manifest in the not infrequent occasions when Haitians felt themselves to have been grossly insulted by Americans of obviously inferior culture.[1]

Despite a turbulent history since their independence, Haitians had kept as a glorifying memory the revolution, which had defeated the forces of Napoleon Bonaparte. And pride that their country was the first black independent nation in the Western Hemisphere. It was again in the name of independence that the northern Cacos took up arms against the Marines and that the elite was laid naked by the racism displayed by the occupiers. Thomas A. Bailey expressed the Haitian reaction to the American occupation in the following terms: "The independence loving Haitian Negroes resented wearing a foreign yoke, especially one imposed by white men ..."[2]

Specific grievances from both the peasants and the elite followed general resentment at the loss of independence. The peasants resented the corvée (forced labor) imposed on them to build roads. In Port-au-Prince, the elite resented the imposition of a "utilitarian" curriculum in their schools. They also looked askance at the intention of the Americans to encourage the formation of a middle class in Haiti.

The Caicos revolted against the corvée and the occupation. Led by Charlemagne Peralte, they used the terrain to wage guerilla war against the Marines. Peralte created a government-in-exile in the north to take over the reign of Haiti following the collapse of the government under the United States. Betrayed, he was killed by a platoon of Marines on October 31, 1919. Peralte's death earned Captain Herman Hanneken the Congressional Medal of Honor. Hanneken had shot the Cacos leader and dealt an irreparable blow to the only armed organization against the occupation. But Peralte's death and the northern peasants' struggle became a rallying point for both Haitians and U.S. groups opposed to the American Occupation.

Already in September 1915, *The Crisis*, the official organ of the National Association for the Advancement of Colored People (NAACP), had published an editorial that began as follows: "Let us save Haiti. Haiti is a noble nation. It is a nation that dared to fight for freedom. This is not the time or place for us American Negroes who seldom have had courage to fight, to point scornful fingers at our brothers."[3]

Following Peralte's death, the NAACP sent its secretary, James Weldon Johnson, to investigate the occupation. Johnson, in a series of articles in *The Nation*, reported to the American public the atrocities committed by the Marines in their "pacification" of Haiti. In one of these articles, Johnson warned that: "The colored people of the United States should be interested in seeing that the independence and sovereignty of Haiti be restored, for Haiti is the one chance that the Negro has in the world to prove that he is capable of self-government."[4]

The new curriculum the U.S. administrators envisaged to introduce in Haitian schools had the potential to affect Haitian society at the core. The Americans perceived that Haiti's economic difficulties lay in its limited agricultural production. To remedy the problem, they offered to transform the country into an agrarian society. They would suspend university education in favor of farming instruction from U.S. teachers. Haitian students preparing to become members of the elite would have to enroll in these classes and earn a living by the sweat of their brows. Thus grew a generation that saw its traditional channel to elite membership threatened.[5] The disinherited generation lay the blame for the chaos and weaknesses, which had resulted in the occupation at the feet of their elders.

Concomitantly with its aim to overhaul Haitian agricultural methods, the U.S. intended to revamp the country's socio-political structure. The election of a National Assembly was suppressed and its functions taken over by a Council of State. The elite bloc bitterly opposed this action, resenting the suppression of the legislature, not only because it was humiliating, but also because it meant loss of income from political positions. Substituting the small appointive Council of State for a Senate and Chamber of Deputies deprived many of them of one of the few respectable means of earning a living.[6] The U.S. considered that changes would favor the evolution of an American-type middle class of traders, managers, salaried professionals and bureaucrats that would counter the influence of the educated elite and the revolutionary tendencies of the peasants.

Thirteen years after the Marines had landed, the peasantry and most of the elite were, for the first time, united—opposition to the American Occupation of their country was the unifying factor. The work of Jean Price-Mars gave direction to the resistance against the occupation.

The vocation of the elite and the first indigenist movement

Jean Price-Mars (1876–1969) was a physician, an ethnologist, a senator, and a diplomat. In 1906 he visited the United States and called on Booker T. Washington whose work at Tuskegee Institute greatly impressed him. During his superintendency from 1912 to 1915 of Haiti's public schools, he advocated Washington's style of technical training for the masses, in addition to the need for courses in agronomy.[7]

Like the ethnologists, Antenor Firmin and Hannibal Price, and other Haitians of his generation, the idea of rehabilitating the black race also affected Price-Mars. Responding to the racialist philosophers Arthur Gobineau and Gustave Lebon, who argued that blacks were incapable of advancement, became Price-Mars's profession. In 1915 while in Paris, he debated Lebon[8] who challenged him to write a book about Haiti.[9] In 1916, he came home to find the elite bewildered in the face of the American occupation.[10] He undertook with a series of conferences—compiled in 1919 under the title *The Elite's Vocation*—a campaign to reinstitute Haitians' civil and political rights the Marines were suppressing. In his conferences, Price-Mars told his audiences that Haitians' ignorance of each other was responsible for the disintegration of the country.

> It is true that when one people does not feel a spontaneous need for a national soul drawn from the intimate solidarity of its diverse classes, by a common aspiration toward a high ideal; when on the contrary, the people are divided into distinct parts—the leading class ignoring the conditions of the masses, the latter ignoring the existence of the former, their only interaction being along economical lines—such people stand on the edge of destruction. It only takes an external threat to its national existence for each class to be driven by its own interests. Finding a common cause is the only thing that can bring them together, to resist one way or another the invasion of their country.[11]

To overcome this moral deficit, Price-Mars proposed that the elite impose on itself a physical and mental "discipline" and pity the masses.[12] "Not as charity...but as a manifestation that it understood and truly accepted its duty."[13] One of the elite, himself, Price-Mars proposed, at the beginning of the American Occupation, that the vocation of his class, whom he accused of "Pilatism" should be generosity toward the masses whom he still considered in 1916 as coming from "backward races." Furthermore, the elite's duty was to give its oligarchic support to the type of education Price-Mars was proposing for the masses. Not the classical education the nation reserved for its select few, but the education found at Hampton Institute and Tuskegee National Institute, which exemplified what can be done for backward races when one knows how to direct them well. It is this kind of education the masses need.[14] In *The Elite's Vocation*, Price-Mars echoed, at times, the fascist philosophy of Sorel and Paeto that was becoming fashionable in Europe.

Fascism was not absent from the aspirations of the young in search of a rallying point to oppose the American Occupation. For example, in the periodical *La Troué* (*The Gap)* which had but one edition, a group of young writers, including a young Jacques Roumain (1907–1944), posted the following manifesto: "We ask above everything else for unity, the term that shines at the head of fascist associations, the fascio that does so much honor to the Duce. We will make him known."[15]

For many years, the educated generation that came of age during the American Occupation searched for a rallying point to oppose foreign rule. They began by denouncing the elder elite that had driven the country to disaster. Concomitantly, they also began in editorials to condemn elite values. Whereas their elders's beacon was the culture and literature of France, the new generation opted for Haiti's own culture in its Caribbean context. Normil Sylvain in *La Revue Indigène (The Indigenist Review*) the first of many periodicals published by the young generation, stated the position of the members. They intended to make their literature a true and living picture of the different manifestations in the life and thoughts of contemporary Haiti. They also intended to give the Haitian point of view in the intellectual, artistic, economic and commercial life of the country. What is more, the word "indigenous" that the elders had made an insulting epithet was to be carried like a banner by the young generation.[16] In the second issue of the *Indigenist Review*, Normil Sylvain elaborated the new character of the "indigenous" Haitian poetry. "If we write in French, we remain foreigners, even barbarians. We do not have to follow refinement of sensibilities or be imitators. We must write about our impressions and express our feelings. Our poems must be translated from the Haitian, the translation of the state of mind and soul that are ours."[17]

To Sylvain, inspiration was in the lullabies of the black nurses who had lulled his generation to sleep. For the first time, Haiti's rich folklore, the sound of the drums, the blowing of the conch and the meringue were to be the source of Haiti's poetry.[18]

The literature of other countries—thus ending France's monopoly—became influential. In the Journal's third issue, Jacque Roumain wrote that it was "natural" to follow the literary design of the French writers. But it was not creative to make them the masters of the "feelings" of Haitian writers as had been the case.[19] He also noted that the flourishing original black literature in the U.S. was being "candidly ignored" in Haiti.[20]

The *Indigenist Review* committed itself, in a tone that often dismayed many of Haiti's older writers, to seek inspiration in the very soul of Haiti and the Caribbean. Jacques Roumain, still very much of the elite, spoke of African-American literature as an example of originality. In 1927, however, the young Haitian writers noticed black literature only superficially. Although the *Review* was regarded as a *committed* periodical, its members were still seeking a central rallying point to give purpose to their effort. Their poetry remained, in spite of their editorials and articles, as trivial and devoid of Haitian originality as had the works of their elders. Moreover, the anthology the group published lacked any mention of the trauma the American Occupation had caused Haiti. But the *Indigenist Review* was a step not only away from the monopoly France held in the cultural and literary life of Haiti, but also a step toward the elite's understanding and acceptance of Haiti's cultural heritage. The periodical also gave prominence to literature in the elite's search for a national Haitian identity as the mobilizing force to oppose the occupation.

Price-Mars: The call for Haitian nationalism

From *The Elite's Vocation* to the publication of *Thus Spoke the Uncle* by Price-Mars, nine years of American Occupation had elapsed. During that time, Price-Mars thoroughly examined Haiti's ethnological foundation in light of studies about Africa done by the European ethnologists Maurice Delafosse[21] and Leo Frobenius.[22] The results were popularized in lectures and articles[23] and compiled in a book published in 1928. *Thus Spoke the Uncle* gave the floundering Indigenist group a focal point to give originality to their literary works and face the American occupation.

The elite had erected a cultural barrier between itself and the masses, partly because of the specter of slavery and the label of uncivilized that hung over Africa. In *Thus Spoke the Uncle*, Price-Mars undertook to rehabilitate culturally the Haitians in the eyes of the elite, by demonstrating that Haiti's folklore was derived from civilizations of which to be proud.

Analyzing the elite's attitude toward the masses, Price-Mars accused them of "collective bovarism." This attitude, he noted, was dangerous because, in being ashamed of one's heritage, the elite could hardly offer any original contribution to human progress. Consequently, Haiti was easy prey to imperialists' designs on its territory.[24] In their efforts to identify themselves as colored Frenchmen, "the elite forgot how to be simply Haitians; men born in determined historical conditions, having in their souls, like any other human group, a psychological makeup that gives the Haitian community its specific features."[25] African, he stated, was the most humiliating name by which one could address a Haitian.

> This country's most distinguished men would rather have some resemblance to an Esquimo, a Samoyede or a Tougawze than to their Guinean or Sudanese ancestry. With what pride some of

> the most representative personalities of our country evoke some bastard affiliation! All the turpitudes of colonial promiscuities, the secret shame of chance meetings, and the brief gamble of two paroxysms have become titles for consideration and glory.[26]

Such aberrations are recipes for a bleak future.[27] Price-Mars again reiterated his views about the impending annihilation of Haiti. "Before the night comes," therefore, he proposes to provide an ethnographical analysis of the Haitian nation in part to respond to the challenge of the racialist Gustave Lebon.

In the first two chapters of *Thus Spoke the Uncle*, Price-Mars examines Haiti's folklore and religious beliefs. It is clear from the stories, legends, and proverbs told to entertain and teach, as well as the popular belief in voodoo, that the culture of the masses derived primarily from Africa. In the next three chapters, Price-Mars studies Africa itself—its philosophical, geographical, historical, and ethnological characteristics—and concludes that Haitians have every reason to be proud of their origin. Did not African empires such as Egypt contribute to the betterment of mankind? he asks.

Chapter seven was devoted to Haitian folklore and literature, arguing against the view that because the elite used the French language as the vehicle of communication its literary production could only be French.[29]

> Who has ever contested the existence of a Swiss, Belgian, Canadian literature of French-expression? Who has even stopped the English language from expressing the soul of African-Americans in the works of James Weldon Johnson, W.E.B. Dubois, Booker T. Washington, and Charles W. Chesnutt? And why would language be an obstacle to Haitians from bringing to the world artistic ideas and a soulful expression that is at the same time very human and very Haitian?[30]

Price-Mars, taking as an example Demesvar Delorme, writes that Delorme's works were totally devoid of any characteristic that would bring to mind his Haitian origin.[31] Delorme sacrificed originality to the worst Haitian prejudice, the belief that Haiti itself did not offer any inspiration to its writers.[32]

To counter the waste of a Delorme's talent, Price-Mars advances a wealth of inspirational material from Haitian legends, proverbs, and stories, which express the Haitian soul.[33]

Unlike *The Elite's Vocation* where the advice is for oligarchic generosity toward the masses, in *Thus Spoke the Uncle,* Price-Mars summons the elite to the school of the original folklore of Haiti, the folklore of the masses. Of this work and of its importance to the movement of Haitian nationalism, which blossomed following its publication, Kleber George-Jacob asserts, "it was the star that was to guide us, to show us the clear luminous path."[34] "It was," according to Robert Cornevin, "the fundamental work that marked the principal date in the national consciousness of the Haitian people." Price-Mars, in the words of Léon Damas, was the "Father of Haitianism."[35]

Besides the importance of *Thus Spoke the Uncle* in giving the elite a focal point in the search for originality, Price-Mars, as a professor of Haitian history at the exclusive Lycée Pétion from 1918 to 1930, instructed a generation in the prerequisite of a Haitian nationalist drive. Among his students and disciples were Francois Duvalier and Dumarsais Estimé, sons of Afro-Haitian parents. They later became presidents of Haiti, via support from the masses against the elite.

With the publication of *Thus Spoke the Uncle*, the first phase of the "indigenist" movement in Haiti came to an end. It was replaced by a militant Haitianism that rose up to ask for an end to the American Occupation. It also opened the way for a resistance literature in which the peasantry and Haiti's cultural heritage became the predominant themes.

The elite's objection to the United States agricultural and other educational programs in Haitian schools laid the basis for effective objection against the occupation itself.[36]

> Conscious of their impotence to change the American supported regime by force, and indignant at being deprived of their constitutional right to elect representatives who would, quite obviously, have proceeded to change it by legislation, the opposition resorted to politically inspired strikes, subversive propaganda, and student demonstrations as the only then available means of expressing their protest.[37]

The "propaganda" was the nationalistic poems which young Haitian writers recited in public to incite the population against the occupation.[38]

On December 7, 1929, the Marines, believing a revolution was in the making, massacred a group of peasants on the way to market. The African American newspaper, *The New York Amsterdam News*, on December 14, 1929, reported that the black population of Harlem demonstrated in the streets and on the steps of City Hall in support of their brethren in Haiti. Throughout the occupation, which lasted until 1934, blacks in America demonstrated, sometimes violently, against it. Almost every issue of *The Crisis* demanded justice for the Black Republic.

The *Save Haiti League*, with affiliation in many states, was founded to protest against American encroachment in Haiti. Many famous African Americans went to Haiti to lend support to the anti-occupation efforts.

Langston Hughes (1902–1967) was among those who traveled to Haiti. He later collaborated with Arna Bontemps in the writing of *Popo and Fifina*, a novel about Haitian children. Hughes also joined Mercer Cook (1903-1987) to translate Jacques Roumain's *Gouverneur de la Rosée* (Master of the Dew). Mercer Cook in turn joined the Haitian diplomat and writer Dantes Bellegarde to produce *The Haitian-American Anthology*.

In 1930 President Herbert Hoover appointed the Forbes Commission to investigate the occupation. The Commission concluded that Haiti's constitution should be restored, providing for an elected legislature. It also recommended a gradual withdrawal of American forces from Haiti. The pull out was completed in 1934. In 1930 the reinstituted National Assembly elected Stennio Vincent, a member of the elite of color, running as a nationalist, president.

In response to Price-Mars' call to relate to the folkloric tradition of their country, in verse and prose, Haiti's writers, beginning in 1931 found inspiration in their Afro-Haitian heritage.

Leon Laleau, with his collection of poems, *Musique Negre*, opened the way for an authentic Haitian poetry of French expression. The collection's most often cited poem, "Treason," was, nevertheless, still written in alternate rhyme, reminiscent of the Romanticists.

This heart that haunts me and doesn't correspond

To my speech and to my dress

And which bites like a crampon,

Feelings and costumes borrowed

From Europe. Can you feel that pain

And that despair unequal to any other.

To tame with French words

This heart which comes from Senegal.[39]

In "Inheritance," also from the *Musique Negre* collection, he writes in alternate rhyming alexandrines. The following stanza speaks of the author's brotherhood with the ancient Maroons.

Certain nights, I listen in me cry the conch,

Which rallied my ancestors in the hill.

I see them again, tired limbs, knife shining,

With murder in their eyes and blood on their dagger.[40]

Leon Laleau, in spite of the recognition to his Afro-Haitian heritage, was a member of the older generation who believed, like many others, that the folkloric themes were restraining the range of Haitian poetry.[41]

Also in 1931 Jacques Roumain's *The Bewitched Mountain* was published with a preface by Price-Mars. It was the first Haitian novel to reflect the pattern described by the latter as necessary for an authentic Haitian literature. "Jacques Roumain," said Price-Mars, "has evoked in some beautiful pages the picturesque and dramatic life of our peasants. From this life, he has marvelously underlined what gave it charm and horror—religious belief."[42]

In *The Bewitched Mountain*, Roumain writes in a language incorporating the Creole of the Afro-Haitians into the French of the educated elite a first accurate glimpse into the lives of the Haitian peasants. Devoid of proselytism, the novel is a continuous description of the Afro-Haitian communal system of clearing the land, of voodoo beliefs and ceremonies and of their stern moral code.

Roumain's social and racial consciousness had evolved considerably since his participation in *La Trouée* and *The Indigenist Journal.* He had become the champion of the Afro-Haitians, not only with his novel, *The Bewitched Mountain,* but also with his political activities for which he was imprisoned several times. Jacques C. Antoine, a friend of Roumain's, said of him that: "He was the leader of the masses, haunted by a vision of a united Haitian people, a vision that dominated his heart and obsessed his mind, the sincerity of the leader who left a life of luxury to become a social menace to his own class. He was responsible for the balance that allowed his peasants to live in him while he lived in them."[43]

Haitianist periodicals and manifestos

The literary renaissance in Haiti was not only expressed in poems and novels with populist characteristics, but also in periodicals and manifestos that opened their pages to the educated elite to convey the values of their new Afro-Haitian consciousness. One of these periodicals was *The Reawakening, (La Relève,)* founded by Jacques C. Antoine in July 1932. In its pages, the writers discussed literary, social and political views and published poems and short stories. Among them was the indefatigable

Price-Mars who, in three successive issues of the *Reawakening*, introduced the Afro-Americans to the elite, their "Negro Renaissance" and its literary production.[44]

In 1934 another group of young writers, expressing an explicit Haitian literature, published the manifesto, *The Tendancy of a Generation*. Here, Haiti's Africanism is advanced to the foreground, "the genius of the race with all its surviving African traits,"[45] as Lorimer Denis puts it.

In 1934 Jacques Roumain gave *Haitianism* a proletarian dimension by founding Haiti's Communist party. The party itself was not effective politically in Haiti; however, Roumain's conversion to Marxism gave his literary works a dimension contrary to the *indigenist* characteristic of his prior efforts involving the peasantry.

In 1938 the first issue of the periodical *The Griots* was published. More Africanist and less politically-oriented than *The Renewal, The Griots* whose co-founders were the group from *The Tendancy of a Generation* and whose director was Carl Brouard published articles echoing Price-Mars' ideas on sociological, anthropological and ethnological subjects regarding the Afro-Haitians. To Carl Brouard, only the masses had the key to Haiti's originality. The *Griots* intended to make their country "the black miracle" as Greece had been the "white miracle." To that end, Brouard stated that:

> "The Haitian griots must sing the splendor of Haiti's landscape … ; the beauty of Haiti's women; the exploits of the ancestors. They must passionately study Haiti's folklore, and remember that to change religion is to venture in an unknown desert, to anticipate one's destiny is to expose oneself to lose the genius and the tradition of one's race."[46]

The *Griots* school revalorized methodically and scientifically, in collaboration with the Haitian Ethnological Institute founded in 1941, the history, the folklore and the voodoo religion of the Afro-Haitians.

But the studies that scrutinized sometimes with a magnifying glass the lives of the Afro-Haitian were, for the most part, less than scientific. Consequently, they provided no benefit to the people observed. Many of these studies were also self-serving as were, for example, the works on voodoo by Lorimer Denis and Francois Duvalier.[47] Jacques Roumain, who also founded the Haitian Ethnological Institute, undertook himself opportune and creditable research on the peasantry. He used his findings to write Haiti's literary masterpieces: *Master of the Dew* and *Ebony Wood.*

What did this period of Haitian nationalism bring to Haiti?

In 1946 the Haitianist movement urged by Price-Mars in response to the elite's *bovarism* and the American Occupation resulted in the elite's and the masses' consciousness of their political strength. In the wake of the "black power" movement that swept over Haiti, Dumarsais Estimé was elected President. The first black president since the American Occupation, he initiated several reforms favorable to the masses: He doubled workers' salaries, initiated a system of social security, provided water and electricity, and protected the religion of the Afro-Haitians against the protests of the Catholic Church. And, too, tourism was given a strong boost. Estimé's presidency, however, lasted but five years. The army led by Paul Magloire overthrew him. Magloire was himself forced to abdicate five years later. Francois Duvalier, exponent of the *Griots* and partisan of Estimé's 1946 revolution, was elected. He had Haiti's constitution changed, making him and his heir presidents for life.

What remains, and is more telling than any other interpretative index of this period which witnessed the elite's drive for Haitian nationalism, is the literary production of the generation that came of age during the 1915 to 1934 American Occupation.

There were two resulting trends from the writers of this period's expression of authenticity. The first dealt with the African characteristics of Haitian culture. The second bore upon the fraternal bond between blacks, elites, workers and peasants. Often, both tendencies would inspire one writer and be reflected in a single work. In poetry, the classical rhyme caesura, enjambement, and hiatus familiar in the works of the elder writers were replaced (except in Jean Brierre's "Here I am Again, Harlem") by highly personal rhyming and rhythmic verse or prose schemes with no set patterns, definite length of lines and stanzas.

Jacques Roumain, in "Guinea": It's the Long Road to Guinea, first published in 1942, speaks mournfully of the Haitian belief in one's return to Africa at death. This famous poem is an example of the understanding of the Haitian peasant's culture that Roumain had achieved at the time of his death in 1944.

It's the long road to Guinea

Death takes you down

Here are the boughs, the trees, the forest

Listen to the sound of the wind in its long hair of eternal night

It's the long road to Guinea

Where your fathers await you without impatience

Along the way, they talk

They wait

This is the hour when the streams rattle like beads of bone

It's the long road to Guinea

No bright welcome will be made for you

In the dark land of dark men

Under a smoky sky pierced by the cry of birds

Around the eye of the river the eyelashes of the trees open on decaying light

There, there awaits you beside the water a quiet village

And the hut of your fathers, and the hard ancestral stone

Where your head will rest at last.[48]

Langston Hughes, the translator, has captured the rhythm of death and personal metaphors of Roumain's French original. The "soul" that has taken "the long road to Guinea" belonged to Roumain himself.

Voodoo fascinated the educated elite of that period to the extent that according to Jacques C. Antoine "they saw in Voodoo the essential source of Haitian art and literature."[49] In the following stanzas, Charles Pressoir described a voodoo ceremony.

One peasant plays the part of Legba,

And like our country women here,

Comes from Ouedo the black one dear,

In a short jacket, sweet Ayida.

But what can be done with a goat without horns?

Next Agoué, the Barkentine,

Lord of the Tempests, Master of Seas

Who cuts off heads, Agou precedes,

A murderous general, menacing, mean.

But what can be done with a goat without horns?

In a corner they roll, they roar,—the big drums

Covered with hairy wild-ass hide,

Monstrous black devils and side by side,

Mama, Papa then Cata comes.[50]

Carl Brouard, in *The Anguished Drum,* made these offerings to the voodoo god, Agouey:

The sky is dark

The wind whistles

And the furious waves

Toss here and there the weak boumba.

Powerful Agouey, have pity on us!

If you deliver us from this peril,

We will give you a green scarf, thick syrups

Succulent cakes made in Port-au-Prince.[51]

Africa, which Price-Mars had revalorized as an integral part of Afro-Haitian culture, also became an inspiring theme to the new generation of Haitian writers. In that light, Arthur Bonhomme, under the pseudonym Claude Fabri, produced this puerile stanza:

I don't know why,

I would like to be tonight

The hirsute ancestor

Who long ago, in the mysterious bush

Danced, ignorant, free and naked.[52]

The Griot, Carl Brouard, more rationally had enunciated the feeling of exile from Africa common to blacks in the following terms:

> Your lost children salute you, maternal Africa. From the Antilles to Bermuda, and from Bermuda to the U.S., they cry for you. They dream of the baobabs, of the blue 'gommiers' full of the flights of the toucans. In the night of their dream, Timbuctou is a mysterious onyx; a black diamond, Abouey or Gao.[53]

They followed the common ancestry premise with the theme of solidarity between blacks, as this poem entitled "Langston Hughes" by Jacques Roumain expresses:

Like a Baedeker your nomad heart wandered

From Harlem to Dakar.

The Sea sounded in your songs—sweet, rhythmic, wild...

And its bitter tears

Of white foam blossom-born.

Now here in this cabaret as the dawn draws near you murmur...

Play the blues again for me!

O! for me again play the blues!

Are you dreaming tonight, perhaps, of the palm trees,

Of black men there who paddled you down the dusks?[54]

And this other dedicated "To Paul Robeson" by Jean Brierre (1909–1992):

One day,

coming out of his gloomy cavern,

shaking off the oppression of centuries and races

still bruised from his chains,

panting for breath

from having borne on his shoulders and in his torn hands

the joys of the world,

the scorn of the world,

the Negro, finding Life again

will transform the sorrowing knells of his heart

into eternal peals of rejoicing.[55]

The most famous solidarity poem written by a Haitian is Brierre's "Harlem, Here I am Again," in remembrance of the men lynched in Georgia in the 1930s:

When you bleed, Harlem, my handkerchief turns red

When you suffer, your lament is in my song

With the same fervor and in the same night,

Black brother, both of us dream of the same thing.[56]

This poem, written in alternate rhyming alexandrine, is an example of the Harlem influence brought about by the American Occupation. Through Harlem, militant Haitian writers such as Brierre and Roumain felt a sense of commonality with African Americans.

To these writers, the perception of having a common oppressor later evolved into the domineering imperialism theme, while the subjugated became the colorless proletariat. It is Jacques Roumain who, in *Ebony Wood* (posthumously published in 1945), wrote the most memorable verses of Afro-Haitian and proletariat duality:

Africa I remember you Africa; you are in me,

like a splinter in a wound,

like a tutelary fetish in the center of the village

make of me the stone of your sling of my mouth the lips of your wound

Of my knees the shattered columns of your abasement...

YET

I only want to be of your race

workers, peasants of all countries.[57]

"New Black Sermon" in which Roumain's personal lyricism found its most intense expression was also published in the *Ebony Wood* collection.

For sheer sincerity and burning denunciation, "New Black Sermon" is a unique call to arms.

Roumain began his long poem with an explanation of how "They" changed Christ— "a poor black man" with a message of peace to the proletariat—into the God of the powerful.

They have made the rich the Pharisees;

The land proprietors, the bankers.

They have made of the bleeding man, the bloody god.

Oh Judas laugh.

Christ between two thieves like a torn flame at the summit of the world

Lighted the revolt of the slaves.

But Christ is today, in the house of the thieves,

And his arms open in the churches the long shadow of the vulture.

And in the caves of monasteries, the priests count the interest on the thirty denarius

And the churches' bells spit death on the hungry multitude.[58]

Roumain then called to the proletariat to rise up in revolt:

We will not forgive them for they know what they do.

They lynched John, who was organizing the union.

They chased him with dogs like a gaunt wolf in the forest.

They hanged him from the trunk of the old sycamore.

No, brothers, comrades.

We will not pray anymore.

Our revolt rises up like the cry of the tempest bird above

The rotten squelch of the swamps.

We will sing no more the sad and desperate spirituals;

Another song gushes out from our throat.

We are deploying our red flags,

Stained with the blood of our just ones.

Under that sign we are marching

Rise up wretched of the earth.

Rise up slaves of hunger.[59]

René Dépestre, born in 1926, was eight years old when the Americans left Haiti. Influenced in literature and politics by the dominant personality of his youth, Jacques Roumain, Depestre at nineteen published *Sparks* in which verses abound with the dual theme of Africa and the proletariat. In "Here I Am," he makes himself and his solidarity with Africa, the Caribbean, the exploited and the proletariat known, in fresh and stirring verses:

Here I am

Citizen of the West Indies

The soul vibrating

I fly in conquest of new bastilles

I gleam in the sunny fields

the harvests of humanity

I question the past

I mutilate the present

I decorate the future

Everything in me aspire to the sun!

Here I am

Son of far away Africa,

Partisan of crazy escapades.

I am looking for the light I am looking for the truth;

I am in love with the soul of my country.

Here I am proletarian;

I feel roaring in me the breath in the crowd.

I feel vibrating in me the rage in the exploited

The blood in black humanity

Bursts my blue veins.

I have melted all the races in my burning heart.

Here I am

Poet,

Adolescent,

Pursuing the great dream of love and beauty.[60]

His next poem, "I Know a Word," emotionally evoked his profound attachment to Haiti:

I know a word that contains all my life

my hopes

my sadness

my nights of tête-à-tête

my colt's leaps

let loose in the savannas of the world

this word gives a sense to my life

it explains the color of my skin

the fatality of my kisses

my hate of compromises

my hands ready

to those who have prostituted their manly duties

this word is my future

this word is my love

this word is my madness—Haiti.[61]

To close the works by poets and novelists of the generation of Haiti's occupation, a poem dedicated to Jacques Roumain, the tragic hero who committed class treason against the Haitian elite of color to lead his peers in search of racial honesty and proletarian solidarity. The poem is by René Dépestre, Roumain's most precocious and loyal disciple:

Comrade Roumain

the blades that your hands have harvested

will not rot in the humid warehouses.

Fraternal and free

pious arms

will tie them in heavy sheaves

to hoist them

all the way to the summits where you soared long ago.

Comrade Roumain

you will germinate

before knowing the dryness

of aborted harvests.

You will germinate in the fertile land of our future

and your thought will flourish and the city of your dreams will flourish too.[62]

And Emile Roumer, who captured a Haitian peasant declaration of love and conveyed it, using gustatory analogies and figures of speech similar to the popular Afro-Haitian style of composing proverbs, stories, and punning, or play on words:

High Yellow of my heart, with breasts like tangerines, you taste better to me than eggplant stuffed with crab, you are the tripe in my pepper pot, the dumpling in my peas, my tea of aromatic herbs. You are the corned beef whose customhouse is my heart my mush with syrup that trickles down the throat. You are a steaming dish, mushroom cooked with rice, crisp potato fries, and little fish fried brown ... My hankering for love follows you wherever you go. Your bum is a gorgeous basket brimming with fruits and meat.[63]

Chapter Fourteen
Paris

Two years after the Marines' occupation of Haiti, a regiment of African Americans arrived in France as part of the U.S. contingent "to make the world safe for democracy." World War I, thus, provided the first opportunity for sustained contact between African Americans and black men of French-ruled Africa, the French West Indies and Guyane, who, themselves, had come to France to defend their mother country. African-American units such as the 369th regiment were incorporated into France's armed forces, adding to the comradeship that developed between African Americans and French-speaking black men. The French demonstrated throughout the conflict sympathy for the plight of African Americans laboring even at the front under Jim Crow rules. Moreover,

> the 369th regiment achieved an outstanding record of valor and distinction in combat. It was the first allied unit to reach the Rhine. And as the first American regiment in the French Army during the war, saw the longest service at the front. It was in the trenches for 191 days. The entire unit was awarded the Croix de Guerre and the Legion of Honor for exceptional bravery in action.[1]

The less blatant racism and the genuine gratitude of the French for their efforts in the war made France welcome to African Americans. Shelby T. McCloy noted that:

> the Negro from far-off America ... was a different person after several months in France, where he was treated by the Whites in a manner he had never known before. Tens of thousands of Negro soldiers had that experience. A few of the privileged were able to return in the years thereafter, but in most instances they merely passed on the word to friends and relatives, who acted on their suggestion of going to France.[2]

These sentiments were factors conducive to the holding of the first Pan-African Congress in Paris in 1919. The deputy from Senegal to Paris since 1914, Blaise Diagne, presided, and the Congress's architect, W. E. B. DuBois, acted as secretary. In addition, there were thirteen participants from Guadeloupe and Martinique, including the deputies, Gratien Candace and Achille-René Boisneuf from Guadeloupe and Joseph Lagrosilliere from Martinique. In 1921, the second Pan-African Congress was in part also held in Paris. From it resulted the formation of the second Pan-African Association whose president was Gratien Candace. Isaac Beton from Martinique was the secretary.

The participation of black American troops in the war made jazz known throughout France. And Lieutenant James Europe's 369th Regiment's band became world famous there.[3] In addition to jazz, African American literature and both Marcus Garvey's and DuBois' movements found wide diffusion in France among black ex-servicemen and students from Africa, the West Indies and Guyane.

The Field Service Fellowship was awarded to a number of black men after the war. This enabled them to study in Paris and other French cities, as well as in London, further lifting the level of contacts between black students from the French empire and those from the U.S. Alain Locke whose *New Negro*, published in 1925, defined the metamorphosis of black Americans after the war, and who is regarded as "the father of the so-called Harlem Renaissance"[4] spent his summer in Paris from 1919 to 1938.[5] Eye-witness reports indicate that following the war, black Americans of all occupations could be seen in cafés and streets of Paris's Left Bank. France was in such vogue that Mercer Cook found it necessary to remind black Americans that it was not Utopia. Because of the African American influx to France, Mercer Cook saw that: "During my last visit to France, in 1938, I was impressed by the surprising facility with which young French Negro intellectuals could quote Langston Hughes, Claude McKay, Sterling Brown, Countee Cullen, and other American Negro authors."[6]

At the same time, so extensive had African American studies become in France that four years after the end of the war, René Maran could state that "the Negro question is a living one. America has made it so."[7] Maran was referring to the upsurge of black American cultural and racial ideas that had found their way to France.

The New American Negro

Following the war, a cleansing mood set in for a short while in American northern cities, inspiring a renewal in black America. Coming back from the European conflict, African Americans as was the case with Africans and West Indians in Paris let it be known in periodicals such as the *Messenger,* the *Crisis,* and *Negro World* that Booker T. Washington's philosophy of accommodation was no longer acceptable. A number of black leaders were now demanding full equality with whites, and, by *1919,* race riots were occurring in a number of American cities. African

Americans rose to oppose Jim Crowism and other racisms. They were, in Claude McKay's poem of rebellion, *If We Must Die*, exhorted not to die like hogs

> hunted and penned in an inglorious spot,
>
> If we must die—oh, let us nobly die!
>
> Like men we'll face the murderous, cowardly pack,
>
> Pressed to the wall dying but fighting back![8]

Concurrently, Harlem, "the largest Negro community in the world" became the American metropolis where—like Paris—a diversity of black peoples and a number of whites influenced each other into giving literature, art and music a fresh vision.

It was the Parisians' newfound love for African American art that reverberated in white America and made Harlem and the "Negro in vogue." Langston Hughes, describing the period when "people were crazy about Negroes," said in this bittersweet passage:

> It was a period when every season there was at least one hit play on Broadway acted by a Negro cast. And when books by Negro authors were being published with much greater frequency and much more publicity than ever before or since in history. It was a period when white writers wrote about Negroes more successfully (commercially speaking) than Negroes did about themselves. It was a period when the Negro was in vogue.[9]

These factors combined to deal a deathblow to the "old" and give birth to the *New Negro* that Alain Locke (1886–1954) documented and interpreted in 1925 as "the transformation of the inner and outer life of the Negro in America that has so significantly taken place in these few years."[10] In *The New Negro: An Interpretation*, Alain Locke set out to provide a self-portrait of black America's artistic expression during the first quarter of the twentieth century. Locke wrote of the "new psychology" that was liberating the black artist from the shackles of imitation, replacing "tutelage" with "self direction." Locke made it clear, however, that the black American artist was following America's democratic ideals—no matter how strident his defiant tone. To Locke, blacks in their migration from the south to the north were also looking, above all else, for a chance at enjoying the democratic principles on which America was founded. He also saw them actively taking part in an upward social march toward the "modern" and more sophisticated region of the country.[11]

As for the new radicalism in African American circles, Locke gave the following interpretation:

> Each generation, however, will have its creed, and that of the present is the belief in the efficacy of collective effort, in race co-operation. This deep feeling of race is at present the mainspring of Negro life. It seems to be the outcome of the reaction to proscription and prejudice; an attempt, and fairly successful on the whole, to convert a defensive into an offensive position, a handicap to an incentive.[12]

Locke's comment found wide appeal among black groups in Paris, demanding full French citizenship. Their periodicals, manifestos and poems echoed his words.

Alain Locke's *The New Negro* gave notice that the new generation of African Americans had a wider horizon and view of their race and its place in America. The *Harlem Renaissance,* the manifestation of the *New Negro*'s vibrant artistic expression, enunciated in literature the freedom of thematic and cultural self-determination. Among the Harlem Renaissance literati of the period who had the most impact on French-speaking blacks in Paris in the 1930s and 1940s was, besides Alain Locke, Claude McKay. His novel *Banjo* written while in France epitomized the new black rebelliousness and sense of exile and embodied the alienation of an educated black man in the white world. Langston Hughes who wrote about the black lower classes in the rhythms of jazz and blues was the most followed. He was the most echoed of the new American Negro Renaissance poets because he exemplified by his personality and his works the descendant of the African slave who was striving for cultural self-determination and full citizenship in a land where he was an outcast. Unlike Haiti, there was no independent black America where the Afro-American was self-governing and in the majority. On the contrary, like the people of the French-speaking West Indies and Guyane, African Americans vied for equality, opposing the inequality of segregation and second-class citizenship. In America, blacks sought redress through American democratic precepts. Langston Hughes, in the 1920s, underlined that African Americans wanted to be an integral part of the U.S. with such poems as "I, Too, Sing America."

> I, too, sing America
>
> I am the darker brother.
>
> They send me to eat in the kitchen

When company comes,

But I laugh,

And eat well,

And grow strong.

Tomorrow,

I'll sit at the table

When company comes. Nobody'll dare

Say to me,

"Eat in the kitchen," then.

Besides,

They'll see how beautiful I am. And be ashamed.[13]

And he spoke for the New American Negro in presenting the manifesto whereby he proclaimed the cultural self-determination of the black American artist:

> We younger Negro artists who create now intend to express our individual dark-skinned selves without fear or shame. If white people are pleased, we are glad. If they are not, it doesn't matter. We know we are beautiful. And ugly too. The tom-tom cries and the tom-tom laughs. If colored people are pleased, we are glad, If they are not, their displeasure doesn't matter either.[14]

Hughes' feelings toward Africa were also representative of blacks in America and the French-speaking West Indies and Guyane. Again, differing from Haiti where the Afro-Haitian's folklore was a reflection of West Africa's culture, African-American folklore, if remaining spiritually African, had been largely Americanized by dint of black Americans "striving to be a co-worker in the Kingdom of culture, to escape both death and isolation ..."[15]

Consequently, Hughes could truthfully state in contemplating Africa: "So long,/ So far away/is Africa." Hughes' refusal to engage in "Primitivism" was also due, as he said, to the fact that "I did not feel the rhythms of the primitive surging through me, and so I could not live and write as though I did. I was an American Negro—who had loved Africa. I was Chicago and Kansas City and Broadway and Harlem."[16]

Chapter Fifteen
The Drive for Full French Citizenship

Paris was the ideal metropolis where intellectuals from all parts of the globe could meet after the war. William L. Shirer, who was a newspaper correspondent stationed there during the inter-war years, described Paris in these terms:

> Paris, the inimitable city, had once again become the cultural capital of the world. Attracted by its beauty, its charm, its civilities, its balmy air of freedom, its appreciation of the life of the mind and the spirit, foreigners flocked to it from all over the world in search of the civilized life which the Parisians already enjoyed.[1]

The budding French Communist Party, in political sympathy with their aspiration for full French citizenship, courted blacks from all parts of the French empire. That made the French capital a center of awareness and possibilities to blacks under French rule. From all accounts, Paris, the most sophisticated city in the world, teemed with ethnic and racial consciousness.

The allies' propaganda against Germany had, in part, created the breach through which blacks from Africa, America, and the Caribbean poured out their political and racial assertions. The allies had proclaimed World War I to be a war to make the world safe for democracy and to ensure the right of all people to self-determination. To demand payment for the lives of the black French subjects who had just died in defense of these ideals, leagues, committees and periodicals sprang up in France after the war.

The two major leagues were the Universal League for the Defense of the Black Race presided over by Tovalou Houeou of Dahomey, and the League for the Defense of the Negro Race led by Tiemoho Garan-Kouyaté and Abdou Koite, both Malians.[2] There was one major committee: The Committee for the Defense of the Negro Race led by the Marxist Lamine Senghor of Senegal.[3] They campaigned in the name of all the black peoples of the empire for an end to second-class status and for full French citizenship. Tovalou Houeou in the July 1924 issue of the Universal League periodical, *The Continents*, expressed his views on citizenship in the following passage:

> We have shed our blood for France as our mother country; now at peace, voluntarily or involuntarily, we continue to fulfill the

citizen's supreme duty of military service. Why do we not enjoy the rights of citizenship? We demand to be citizens, whatever the country. If France rejects us, we ask for autonomy. If she welcomes us, we ask for total assimilation and integration.[4]

In November 1931, Paulette Nardal of Martinique, who also held a literary salon for black intellectuals passing through Paris, and Leo Sajou of Haiti founded in Paris a leading bi-lingual periodical to voice demands for equality and cultural self-determination. *The Journal of the Black World* was a politically moderate publication with Catholic leanings. Its importance rested on its goal, "to give to the intellectual elite of the black race and to the Friends of black peoples an organ to publish their artistic, literary and scientific works."[5] Sajou's Haitian connection seems to have been purely incidental. Only two articles concerning his homeland were published in the *Journal.*

In its first issue, the editorial entitled, "What We Want To Do," expressed the pan-black scope of the periodical and the intention to underline the African link between blacks and "to create between [them] without distinction of nationality an intellectual and a moral link, enabling them to know each other better; to love each other fraternally, in order to defend their collective interests and to illustrate their race."[6]

The works of European ethnographers about Africa, such as Leo Frobenius, were bearing fruits. The editorial noted, for example, that the periodical intended "to study and make known through the press, books, conferences, and in the schools all about Negro civilization and the natural riches of Africa, the motherland three times sacred to the black race." Subsequently, the Journal published extracts from the works on Africa by Maurice Delafosse and Leo Frobenius.

The *Journal* also published works by Claude McKay, Langston Hughes, and Alain Locke. Aimé Césaire, who a few years later founded his own periodical to speak of negritude, reacquainted himself with these Afro American writers whom he would echo.[7]

Concurring with Fanon and the theme in Oruno Lara's *The Color Line*, Paulette Nardal, in the last issue of the *Journal* examined the influence of one's exile in the awakening and acknowledgement of one's racial consciousness. She admitted, "For the consciousness of one's race to be awakened in a number of West Indians it was necessary for them to leave their little country."[8] She explained that the sensation of being "uprooted while in the mother country...pushed the West Indian to implant himself further into his race."[9] Bigotry in the mother country and the meeting with blacks from America and Africa created a critical mass of commitment to seek acknowledgement and redress.

The Revolt of *Self Defense*

The "profound reflection and arousal to revolt" in the racially and politically charged atmosphere of 1930s Paris spilled over in the pages of a periodical devoted to the destruction of the French bourgeoisie of color. Founded in June 1932 by a group of students of color from Martinique—a number of who had written for the *Journal* that they later thought too moderate—proclaimed the class-suicide mission of its founders. Its editorial told readers that *Self Defense (Légitime Défense)* was a warning, devoted, as it was, to fight "those who are not suffocated by this bourgeois, Christian Capitalist World."[10] Its founders believed in two ideologies, Marxism and Surrealism. About Marxism they wrote, "We believe without reserve in the triumph of the [third International], because we side with the dialectical materialism of Marx victoriously submitted to the test by Lenin."[11] Leopold Sedar Senghor, in his *Négritude et Marxisme,* recalls this period of intense recruitment efforts by the West Indian Communists.

> Indeed, right from the time of our arrival in Europe, we were submitted to Marxist propaganda. Some black students—especially the West Indians —had succumbed to its seduction. And they tried in turn to seduce us. They presented 'scientific socialism' as the final solution to our problems.[12]

On surrealism they said, "We accept equally without reservation surrealism, to which, in 1932, we attach our becoming."[13] Readers were asked to read André Breton's surrealist manifesto, the works of Louis Aragon, René Crevel, Salvador Dali, Paul Eluard, Benjamin Peret, Tristan Tzara, Sade, Hegel, Lautreamont, Rimbaud, to cite a few.[14] (The *Self Defense* banner came from Breton's manifesto.)

Self Defense also evoked the works of Freud, which had helped liberate the subconscious from the restrictions of a stifling society and had directly influenced Dadaism and Surrealism. From the vintage precepts of Surrealism, *Self Defense* criticized the West Indian writers of color. In one of its articles, for example, René Ménil (1907–2004) proposed that "the Black West Indian writer recognize first of all his own passions and express only himself—that he take the opposite direction of the useful, i.e., the path of dream and poetry."[15] Then, according to Ménil, he "would find fantastic images of which the African...statuettes were forms of expression."[16] He would also find the poems, the stories, and the jazz of African Americans in addition to the works of the French Dadaists and Surrealists.[17]

In an article on poetry entitled "Poor Poetry," Etienne Léro, the initiator of *Self-Defense* and the movement's leader, affirmed that:

> It was inaccurate to speak of a West Indian poetry. The majority of the population did not read or write in French. Some people of color, intellectually and physically bastardized, literally rotten by white decadence, have made themselves, to the French bourgeoisie that use them, ambassadors of the masses, whom, they suffocate and deny, because too dark.[18]

In the West Indies, "the poet is recruited exclusively from the class which has the privilege of education and is well to do."[19] Consequently, "characteristics of the poetry's mediocrity is clearly tied to the existing social order."[20] Etienne Léro turned to black America to create a poetry attuned to social realities in the French West Indies. He states:

> The wind from black America will quickly, we hope, clean our West Indies from its stunted fruits of a sick culture. Langston Hughes and Claude McKay, the two black revolutionary poets have brought us, preserved in red alcohol, the African love of life, the joy of African love, the African dream of death.[21]

Next to Léro's article were quotes from McKay's *Banjo* depicting a Martiniquan student of color alienated from race and culture. Léro promoted in the same breath the Russian Revolution and Mahatma Gandhi as examples to follow.

Because of its virulence, its dedication through Marxism and Surrealism to be detrimental to the colored bourgeoisie of the French West Indies, in addition to the curse to all student periodicals—shortage of funds, *Self Defense* had only one issue. That issue, however, had incorporated all the new tendencies that had burst on the Parisian cultural and political scene after the First World War. Armed with these new penchants, dynamically, and with determination and abundant youthful enthusiasm, the *Self Defense* movement declared war on the society whence it came. The fact that *Self Defense* was published at all demonstrates the level of racial and political consciousness at work within the new generation of students from the French West Indies, Guyane, and Africa who, like so many others before them, had come to France for their schooling in order to take their place in the colonial hierarchy.

The commentaries and works of those who responded to its message of rebellion reveal the far-reaching influence of *Self Defense*. Deserving of note, because he co-founded a periodical and was the first to publish a literary work in the manner Etienne Léro proposed, was Léon Gontran Damas.

Fifteen years after the publication of *Self Defense* during which time its revolutionary line had made great strides, Damas retrospectively wrote of Léro:

> He marked a stage, a metamorphosis through which all those who understood and agreed with his message committed themselves totally to their individual adventure. What he attempted has already produced real rewards. Beginning with his poems...a poetry was born...It is to him and to no one else that the colonial poetry of French expression owes its new blood and a chance at salvation. It is to him and to no one else that it owes to have taken since 1932 the dream road.[22]

In reading Aimé Césaire's and Léon Damas's works, it is clear how extensively Césaire responded to René Ménil's surrealist call and Damas to Langston Hughes's racial beliefs echoed by Etienne Léro. Nevertheless, this periodical with the "revolutionary tone" never proposed or even hinted at a break with France itself. On the contrary, by carrying the banner of the French Communist party, it reinforced the political assimilationist drive of the French West Indies and Guyane, which the party promoted.

The Jacobins of France had, since the 1789 Revolution—congruent with their interests—supported the political aspirations of men such as Bissette and Barbes. As the drive for full French citizenship intensified during the period between the first and second world wars, the Jacobins, who had become in the 1920s and 30s the trade unionists of the Communist-led union C.G.T. *Confédération générale du travail* and C.G.T.U *Confédération générale du travail unitaire*, supported, again openly, the aspirations of the people under French-rule in the West Indies and Guyane. The French Communist party was motivated at that time in its support and recruitment of colonials by one overriding factor: the rise of fascism in Europe.

In France, the fear of Bolshevism was manifested in turn by the formation in 1927 of extreme right royalist movements such as the Cross of Fire. These movements opposed not only organized labor unions such as the C.G.T. and C.G.T.U. but also the republic itself and its Rights of Man. Speaking of rightist movements in France during the inter-war years, British historian, David Thomson remarked, "Taken altogether, they provided all the elements of propaganda, private army and mystique, which in Germany, Italy, and elsewhere produced Fascist revolutions. And between 1934 and 1936, all the circumstances favorable to a Fascist revolution co-existed in France."[23]

The rising fascist tide compelled the French socialist and radical parties to forego their ideological differences and link their forces into a Common Front in the spring of 1932. It was no coincidence that *Self Defense* also saw light in 1932 and disappeared the year the Radical Socialist Front exited.

As the growth of fascism continued unabated, the communist unions staged protest demonstrations, and, from 1932 to 1936, pitched battles occurred between their adherents and the Cross of Fire's supporters. Concurrently, the economic depression ravaging the U.S. and the European countries hit France in the early 1930s, further aggravating the Third Republic's political crisis. From 1930 to 1935, there were two succeeding governments in France, and on July 14, 1935, to save the republic "against the imminent threat of the fascist leagues," the radicals again joined the socialists in a Common Front pact under the watch slogan of "the Jacobins 1789 Revolution." Prodded by Moscow,[24] the French Communist Party shelved its abhorrence of the socialists and joined them and the radicals in a Popular Front arrangement in 1935, ensuring success at the polls in 1936.

Many blacks from the West Indies, Guyane, and elsewhere were drawn, like *Self Defense*, into supporting and joining forces with the sworn enemy of fascism, the communists. The overwhelming reason for their support was that in the French West Indies the line was also drawn between the white Creoles who had aligned themselves with the fascists and the blacks and the people of color who benefited from communist support against the Creoles. In January 11, 1934, the Creoles assassinated André Aliker, head of the Communist Party in Martinique. In addition, the opposition of the Soviet Union and the French Left to the occupation of Abyssinia by Fascist Italy further drove a number of French blacks to side of the communists. The occupation of the Rhineland by Germany and the plight of the republicans in the Spanish Civil War sealed their adherence to the belief that communism was the only force against fascism, imperialism's offshoot.

The support the left received from the colonies to fight the rightists was instrumental in furthering the full citizenship aspirations of colonial blacks. For example, the Popular Front government promoted Felix Eboué to the governorship of Guadeloupe. He was governor as long as the Front was in power in France—two years.

The advent of the Popular Front to power was further conducive to the publication of a number of periodicals dedicated to highlighting the views and the expectations of colonial blacks. Among these was *The Black Student: Monthly Journal of the Association of Martinican Students in France* (*L'Etudiant Noir: Journal Mensuel de l'Association des Etudiants Martiniquais en France*).

Chapter Sixteen
The Enunciation of Negritude—The New French Negro

According to Léon Damas, it was Aimé Césaire of Martinique, a student in Paris since 1931, whose idea it was to create in 1935 a periodical after *Self Defense* had folded. *The Black Student*, a monthly, would introduce the anti-assimilationist precepts of an association of French-speaking West Indian, Guianese and African students in Paris.[1] Except for the Guianese Damas, the other students were from the two most assimilated territories in the empire, Martinique and Senegal. These students, as their names appeared on the periodical's front page, were A. Césaire of Martinique, L. Damas of Guyane, B. Diop of Senegal, O. Soce of Senegal, A. Maugée of Martinique, L. Sainville of Martinique, and L. Senghor of Senegal. The founding of *The Black Student,* which, because of the customary financial crunch, was published only five times, starting in March 1935,[2] was one more manifestation of the wave of racial consciousness and cultural self-determination movements that were taking place all over the black world during the inter-war years.

Unlike the *Self Defense* faction who determined communism and surrealism as the two basic ideologies for their revolution, *The Black Student* group, albeit, not totally rejecting these two ideologies, stressed instead their African cultural link. *The Black Student* was then the instrument through which a number of students from France's colonies—never rejecting France itself—proposed to defend their black cultural self-determination against the total immersion into French culture that their elders had upheld. This quest for cultural autonomy was the expression in French of Locke's enunciation and analysis of the "New Negro. "It was equally an echo in French of the views of Langston Hughes stating that, "we younger Negro artists who create now intend to express our individual dark-skinned selves without fear or shame."[3] It was from the concept of the "dark-skinned self" that Césaire formulated his notion of Negritude. Césaire who had studied English with Damas in Martinique under Gilbert Gratian and whose thesis was on African American literature[4] probably came upon the term in an American dictionary, perhaps during one of his translations of a black American poet. The term, which did not exist in French, was Negrohood.[5]

The noun-forming suffix, "hood" is translated in Latin as "tudo," which denotes a state, a condition, a quality, a characteristic; for example, womanhood, the distinctiveness of a woman. Negrohood or negritude, in turn, denotes the uniqueness distinguishing the Negro. The above meaning of the term negritude is the one Césaire himself used in explaining the word. Other meanings of negritude first appeared in Jean-Paul Sartre's *Black Orpheus*, the preface to Léopold Senghor's 1948 *Anthology of the New Black and Malagasy Poetry (Anthologie de la nouvelle poésie nègre et malgache)*. The meaning Sartre gave to Negritude, Senghor and others extrapolated to interpret an African way of being and speak of a movement.[6]

Césaire used the term *negritude* for the first time in an article published in *The Black Student's May-June 1935 (L'Etudiant Noir, Première Année. ... N. 3 Le Numéro : 1 franc MAI-JUN 1935)*. Under the general heading, *Thoughts (Les Idées),* and the sub-heading *Black Affairs* (*Nègrerie*), and the title "Racial Consciousness and Social Revolution" ("Conscience Raciale et Revolution Sociale") (see illustrations pp. 122–123). The West Indian "*must tear himself from superficial values; take possession of his most immediate black self [and] plant his négritude as one does a beautiful tree until it bears its most authentic fruits." (...déchirer les superficielles valeurs, saisir en nous le nègre immédiat, planter notre négritude comme un bel arbre jusqu'à ce qu'il porte ses fruits les plus authentiques*). However, only in his *Return to My Native Land* published in 1939 that, among his literary works, he uses the term freely. An analysis of its usage in that work gives further evidence to the meaning ascribed to it by Césaire. He uses it in *Return*—first in connection to Haiti's declaration of independence in 1804: "Haiti, where négritude stood up for the first time and said it believes in its humanity." Haiti, where the African spirit demonstrated its humanity through revolt against slavery. Concerning features and color characteristics, Césaire states in another passage, "his nose seemed a peninsula adrift, his very négritude paled under the action of a tireless tawing."[7] The condition and the living qualities of Césaire's Negrohood found expression in these lines: "My négritude is not a stone, its deafness thrown against the clamor of the day, my négritude is not a speck of dead water on the dead eye of the earth, my négritude is neither a tower nor a cathedral."[8] Again, each of the negritude terms used in the above excerpts can be replaced by the term Negrohood or Negro humanhood.

Négritude has also known slavery:

> And the determination of my biology no longer imprisoned by a facial angle, by the texture of hair, by a nose sufficiently flattened, by a sufficiently melanin tint, and négritude neither a cephalic index, or a plasma, or a soma, but measured with the compass of suffering.[9]

Aimé Césaire, or as he described himself and as they call him in Martinique, le Nègre fondamental, *circa 1972, in a side office at his city hall where he was mayor from 1945 until 2001. Césaire who dominated the politico-cultural French speaking Caribbean space for most of the 20th century was even more popular there than De Gaulle in his day, ensuring that Martinique, Guadeloupe, and Guyane would become and remain counties and then regions of France. Paradoxically, no one—not even his student, Frantz Fanon—denounced colonialism with more fervor and with more grace than Césaire did. Admitting the contradiction, he suggested that his poetry was revenge on his politics. He spoke French so well that someone said of him,* "quand Césaire parle, la grammaire française sourit," *when Césaire speaks French grammar smiles. He condemned one of France's colonization schemes as "genocide through substitution," but told French Prime Minister François Fillon on January 5, 2008,* "Nous [la Martinique, les Antilles] sommes le symbole de quelque chose, le symbole de la vieille France, de la vieille politique, de l'espérance et de l'avenir ... *Nous avons besoin de vous car c'est grâce à vous que nous survivons." He thought assimilation, France's cultural credo, inimical to* egualité; *but unlike Fanon, he never envisaged one's self-determination to guarantee that equality. His children rejected calls to transfer his remains to the Pantheon in Paris.*

Césaire would forever be known as the father of the 1946 French law conferring the status of Départements *(counties) upon Guyane, Guadeloupe and Martinique. This weighed heavily on him, and he had to defend himself later against charges of naiveté or even of having sold out. He himself had questions as to what would remain of the identity of his Caribbean region—even what the ancestors would think after Guyane, Guadeloupe and Martinique were annexed into a greater French nation. Césaire said he revised his vocabulary and went along, explaining that he was aware that was what the masses wanted for their countries—to be* départements *of France. That was the will of his constituents. That was, they believed, their ticket to social justice and to equality. To be sure, Haiti's self-determination failure had marked Césaire; he gambled that French administration would protect the* old colonies *from a similar fate. Then, too, was the genuine apprehension that the old French colonies of the Caribbean would fall under the control of the United States, which, among black students in Paris at the time, was considered the hotbed of lynching and racism.*

In L'Etudiant Noir, Volume 1, number 3 (May-June), *shown on pages 123 to 128, Aimé Césaire uses the word negritude for the first time. Perhaps most interestingly is his 1935 translation of the communist poem* Black Hands *by Richard Wright, the writer who, in the author's opinion, had the most influence on Césaire. (The author was carrying the ashes of Léon Damas to Guyane with a stopover in Martinique and told Césaire who was meeting him at the airport about the cremation that he had witnessed in Washington. Césaire in turn told the author about his own experience of taking his friend, Richard Wright's remains, to be cremated eighteen years earlier in Paris. "I could hear the bones explode," he recounted.)*

Première Année ... N. 3. Le Numéro : 1 franc MAI-JUIN 1935

L'Étudiant noir

Journal Mensuel de l'Association des Étudiants Martiniquais en France

Administration et Rédaction : 20, rue Duranton - PARIS-15e

ABONNEMENTS { FRANCE et COLONIES 12 fr. ETRANGER .... 15 fr.

SOMMAIRE

LES IDÉES

Nègreries

Conscience Raciale et Révolution Sociale

Le matérialisme ne dit point que les pensées ne sont pas efficaces, mais seulement que leurs causes ne sont pas des pensées. Que leurs effets ne sont pas des pensées. (Nizan. Les Chiens de garde).

Quelle révolution fut jamais faite par le monde innocent des curiosités ? Qui soulèvera jamais un joujou contre son propriétaire ? Pourtant, c'est bien là le tour de force que veulent entreprendre nos révolutionnaires nègres lorsqu'ils demandent au nègre de se révolter contre le capitalisme qui l'opprime. Le moyen, en effet d'appeler autrement qu'un joujou un peuple d'assimilés ? Dostoïewsky le disait déjà, ou peu s'en faut : Toute race qui croit qu'elle n'a rien à dire au monde n'est qu'une « curiosité ethnique » et tout individu est un joujou qui croit qu'au rendez-vous du recevoir et du donner, son peuple arrive les mains vides.

« Agissez », dit-on au nègre. Mais comme agir c'est créer, et comme créer c'est pétrir et faire lever sa naturelle substance, le nègre [illegible] : nous n'agira point, qui se distrait de lui et vit à part soi.

Un mal étrange nous ronge, en effet, aux Antilles : une peur de soi-même, une capitulation de l'être devant le paraître, une faiblesse qui pousse un peuple d'exploités à tourner le dos à sa nature, parce qu'une race d'exploiteurs lui en fait honte dans le perfide dessein d'abolir « la conscience propre des exploités ».

Les exploiteurs blancs nous ont donné, à nous autres exploités noirs, une culture, mais une culture blanche, une civilisation, mais une civilisation blanche, une morale, mais une morale blanche, nous paralysant ainsi par mailles invisibles pour le cas hypothétique où nous nous libérerions du plus sensible esclavage matériel qu'ils nous ont imposé. Et ils ourdissent leur trame, patiemment, inlassablement, par ruse diligente jusqu'à ce que nous mourions à la connaissance de nous-mêmes.

Dès lors, s'il est vrai, que le philosophe révolutionnaire est celui qui élabore les techniques de libération, s'il est vrai que l'œuvre de la dialectique révolutionnaire est de détruire « toutes les perceptions fausses prodiguées aux hommes pour voiler leur servitude », ne devons-nous pas dénoncer l'endormeuse culture identificatrice et placer sous les prisons qu'édifia pour nous le capitalisme blanc, chacune de nos valeurs raciales comme autant de bombes libératrices ? Ils ont donc oublié le principal ceux qui disent au nègre de se révolter sans lui faire prendre d'abord conscience de soi, sans lui dire qu'il est beau et bon et légitime d'être nègre.

Ils ont oublié de parler au nègre le seul langage qu'il puisse légitimement entendre, puisque, différent en cela de « l'employé du bureau de M. Gradgrind », « l'esclave nègre » a le sang riche encore d'affections humaines et que c'est d'une affection humaine, comme le fait remarquer Chesterton, qu'il aimera la fidélité ou la liberté.

La vérité est que ceux qui prêchent la révolte au nègre n'ont pas foi dans le nègre et que dans leur fierté d'être révolutionnaires, ils oublient qu'ils sont nègres, premièrement et toujours : esclavage encore et de la plus stérile espèce.

Le héros de Paul Morand, « l'assimilé » Occide est révolutionnaire lui aussi : grâce à lui, Haïti a ses Soviets, Port-au-Prince devient Octobreville, bel avantage s'il reste prisonnier des blancs, singe stérilement imitateur !

Tant pis pour ceux qui se contentent d'être des Occide, par mépris de ce qu'ils appellent du « racisme ». Pour nous, nous voulons exploiter nos propres valeurs, connaître nos forces par personnelle expérience, creuser notre propre domaine racial, sûrs que nous sommes de rencontrer en profondeur, les sources jaillissantes de l'humain universel.

Ainsi donc, avant de faire la Révolution et pour faire la révolution, — la vraie —, la lame de fond destructrice et non l'ébranlement des surfaces, une condition est essentielle : rompre la mécanique identification des races, déchirer les superficielles valeurs, saisir en nous le nègre immédiat, planter notre négritude comme un bel arbre jusqu'à ce qu'il porte ses fruits les plus authentiques.

Alors seulement, nous aurons conscience de nous ; alors seulement, nous saurons jusqu'où nous pouvons courir seuls ; alors seulement nous saurons où le souffle nous manque, et parce que nous aurons saisi notre particulière différence, et que nous « jouirons loyalement notre être », nous pourrons triompher de tous les esclavages, nés de la « civilisation ».

Etre révolutionnaire, c'est bien ; mais pour nous autres nègres, c'est insuffisant ; nous ne devons pas être des révolutionnaires accidentellement noirs, mais proprement des nègres révolutionnaires, et il convient de mettre l'accent sur le substantif comme sur le qualificatif.

C'est pour cela qu'à ceux qui veulent être révolutionnaires uniquement pour pouvoir se moquer du nègre au nez « suffisamment

Page one of volume 1, number 3 issue (May-June) of L'Etudiant Noir *shows its masthead.*

aplati » ; c'est pour cela qu'à ceux qui croient en Marx uniquement pour passer la ligne, nous disons :

Pour la Révolution, travaillons à prendre possession de nous-mêmes, en dominant de haut, l'officielle culture blanche « gréement spirituel » de l'impérialisme conquérant.

Attelons-nous courageusement à la besogne culturelle, sans craindre de tomber dans un idéalisme bourgeois, l'idéaliste étant celui qui considère l'idée comme fille d'idée et comme matrice d'idées, quand nous y voyons, nous, une promesse qui ne peut pas ne pas s'épanouir en un buissonnement d'actes.

Oui, travaillons à être nègre, dans la certitude que c'est travailler pour la Révolution, car celui-là fera la Révolution qui sera dans sa force, et celui-là est dans sa force qui est dans son véritable caractère.

Aimé CESAIRE.

Racisme ? Non, mais Alliance spirituelle

« C'est son passé même qui doit conditionner son devenir ».

[A. GIDE].

On nous accuse de racisme, mes amis et moi. Quoi d'étonnant ? C'est le mot du jour, et le meilleur moyen de rallier le troupeau. Ménalchas, le nègre au sourire discret, me soufflait à l'oreille : « Nous autres, nègres, nous devons être... conformistes ». Mais on se garde bien de définir le racisme, de citer les textes qui nous confondront. C'est tellement scolaire !...

Le raciste croit sa race supérieure, qu'elle est seule à posséder la vérité, et qu'étant, par le fait, au-dessus des communes lois de l'humanité, elle a le droit, le devoir d'imposer sa domination par tous les moyens. Racisme est ennemi de « complexe d'infériorité », mais son frère ennemi. Il y a erreur, préjugé de part et d'autre, mais opposition fondamentale.

Et c'est pourquoi se contredisent ceux qui nous accusent d'être racistes et « complexés ». Il est vrai qu'ils sont gens subtils et entendus. La conscience d'une certaine infériorité peut-être à l'origine d'un mouvement raciste, je le concède. C'est même ce qui s'est produit dans l'après-guerre pour le racisme allemand, pour le nationalisme chinois. Qui ne sait qu'il y a là conscience et non sentiment ? Car il y a bien infériorité momentanée et actuelle sur un domaine limité, non infériorité essentielle et permanente. Je le répète, il y a antinomie entre racisme et complexe d'infériorité, et nous rejetons l'un et l'autre.

— Qu'êtes-vous donc ?

— Des nègres, des nègres qui vivent, qui veulent agir; car nous avons conscience de nos défauts et de nos qualités. Et vivre, c'est résoudre les problèmes de l'heure, combler les trous : « Qui saute et tombe dans le feu », dit Duolof M'Diage, « doit faire un autre saut ».

L'humanité est un orchestre ; nous avons la section rythmique. Ou si vous préférez, c'est la poste d'autrefois. Elle a des relais établis de distance en distance. La race noire a pris le harnais jadis ; aujourd'hui, c'est de nouveau son tour.

De grands savants soutiennent que les premières civilisations qui naquirent, étaient des civilisations noires. Pour nous en tenir aux époques historiques, de grands empires nègres ont fleuri en Afrique au Moyen-Age. Les voyageurs arabes qui visitaient le Soudan, s'émerveillaient de leur splendeur et de leur prospérité. A les en croire, ces états ne le cédaient en rien à ceux de la Méditerranée. Je ne veux citer pour mémoire, que le fameux Empire du Mali, qui s'étendait de la bouche du-Niger à l'Atlantique, et qui atteignit son apogée au XIXe siècle, sous le règne de Jougo Moussa, dont la réputation de grand guerrier, d'habile administrateur et de sage justicier, était connue de Séville à Constantinople. C'est alors que l'Université de Tombouctou la Rouge, attirait jusqu'aux savants de l'Afrique du Nord.

Au moment où cette civilisation prenait un vigoureux essor intellectuel, arrivèrent, comme dit le grand africanisant Delafosse, « les barbares du Nord » qui, armés d'armés à feu inconnues des nègres, misent tout à feu et à sang. La décadence commença, aggravée par des bouleversements climatériques qui desséchèrent la région des savanes et isolèrent les nègres. Mal et bien. Il y eut sommeil intellectuel, — moins profond qu'on ne le croirait, et c'est merveille d'entendre nos paysans discuter en rivalisant de bon sens et de finesse. Mais les nègres, à l'abri du désert et des forêts, purent conserver intactes leur beauté plastique, leurs richesses artistiques et morales.

Que voulons-nous aujourd'hui ? Réveiller la race, si elle n'est déjà réveillée, et la jeter dans le combat que mène l'humanité contre les forces de destruction. A la vieille Europe, nous voulons apporter des éléments neufs d'humanité. Ces éléments, il nous faut les découvrir en nous, et, pour cela, perfectionner l'instrument de notre raison.

Ainsi donc, nous prônons l'échange, « l'alliance spirituelle », selon la belle expression de M. Brévié. Recevoir et donner : tout est là. Infériorité ou supériorité ? Je préfère dire : différence, féconde, et ici, il n'y a pas commune mesure.

Ils le savent bien, nos détracteurs, que nous ne sommes ni racistes ni « complexés ». Voilà précisément pourquoi, reprenant une vieille méthode, ils attaquent pour ne pas être attaqués. On cherche mille prétextes pour trahir, on accumule sophismes et contradictions. Que ne serait-on pour ne pas être nègre ? On est slavophile, anglais, esquiman ; on se fait l'esclave soumis de tel ou tel « isme » qui, croit-on, vous donne des yeux bleus. Du haut du morne, on contemple avec une pitié non exempte de candeur les « pauv' nég' guinains » de la plaine. Mais eux savent qu'ils sont forts et beaux, et chantent au soleil levant.

Aux camarades de droite — l'expression est commode — j'ai répondu précédemment, me plaçant sur leur propre terrain. Mais ce sont gens coriaces, et je les renvoie aux matraqueurs professionnels.

Certains camarades de gauche me disent : il y a un problème de classe, pas de race. Que ne disent-ils plutôt qu'il y a un problème de race doublé d'un problème de classe. Car aux Antilles, la race préexiste à la classe, et l'explique à l'origine. Le problème étant double, la solution doit aussi l'être. Bien plus on ne doit résoudre le conflit de classe qu'en vue de conserver les valeurs — mais seules, les valeurs humaines — de chaque race, donner du pain au peuple blanc et au peuple noir pour leur permettre à chacun, de vivre sa culture propre, fécondée par des apports nouveaux.

C'est ce qui explique que nous ne sacrifions pas la Culture à la Politique. Vous négligez le spirituel pour l'économique. Celui-ci est important, soit. Mais quand vous aurez fait la révolution, quel pain spirituel donnerez-vous au peuple noir, à qui vous aurez fait perdre son originalité ? Car il est plus facile de perdre ses qualités originelles que d'en acquérir d'autres — un grand écrivain métropolitain en faisait la remarque sur notre bourgeoisie de couleur. Il est à craindre qu'il n'ait alors pris l'instrument pour la fin, qu'il ne se soit attaché à la politique et à la haine pour elles-mêmes et que, n'ayant plus de bourgeois à dévorer, il ne déchire ses propres entrailles après avoir mangé ses dirigeants.

Politique si vous voulez. Mais culture aussi. Regardons l'Amérique noire. En dix ans, ce que nos politiciens appellent ses « littérateurs » ont su acquérir le respect et la sympathie du monde pensant à leurs valeurs raciales. C'est Paul Morand qui l'affirme. Une nation, une race ne se libère que par elle-même ; car progrès suppose identité. « Elle se doit », écrit A. Gide, « de prouver qu'elle est capable d'évoluer sans pour cela renier son passé. Un renouveau qui s'achèterait à ce prix serait l'équivalent d'une faillite. C'est son passé même qui doit conditionner son devenir ».

L. SEDAR SENGHOR.

Au Congrès mondial des Ecrivains.

La délégation Antillaise

Nous reproduisons la déclaration qui a été lue au Congrès Mondial des Ecrivains, au nom de la délégation antillaise.

Ce texte qui a obtenu un vif succès représente assez exactement notre position, celle que nous n'avons jamais cessé de défendre dans l'Etudiant Noir.

A noter cependant une légère contradiction, puisque l'auteur qui parle, au début, de la race comme un mythe, en reconnait implicitement la réalité, quand il affirme plus loin ne pas vouloir « Se faire une blancheur. »

L'écrivain, à l'heure actuelle et quelle que soit sa race et sa nationalité ne peut se résigner à prôner des valeurs de fondement uniquement individualiste sous peine d'inefficacité. Et comme nul écrivain ne peut accepter sans hypocrisie l'idée que sa pensée soit inefficace, il sera réduit à masquer cette inefficacité par le bluff, s'il ne tente pas sans arrière-pensée d'entrainer derrière un idéal qui soit en même temps le sien tout un peuple. Mais cela suppose que ses aspirations personnelles composent avec l'immense volonté populaire, car le peuple sait de plus en plus, ce qu'il veut.

Nous, écrivains d'origine antillaise, petit-fils d'esclaves noirs et quelquefois aussi d'aventuriers blancs, dont même l'aspect physique est souvent un pur défi au mythe de la race, nous sommes fiers d'accorder notre jeune voix, aux grandes voix de la liberté, de l'authentique revendication humaine qui s'expriment dans ce congrès. La particularité de nos origines commande que nous attachions à la culture une valeur éminente, car elle nous a transformés en peu de temps, bien que, attachés par mille liens aux peuples qu'on appelle primitifs, la liberté et la fantaisie ont gardé pour nous une importance vitale. Nous acceptons notre propre forme, comme la vie, avec joie et nous refusons une assimilation qui serait une réduction et une mutilation. Au rebours de certains, nous ne voulons pas, à force de conformisme nous faire une blancheur. Nous savons que la Russie Soviétique n'a pas hésité à se faire l'institutrice du globe le jour où elle a consacré toutes les particularités ethniques et toutes les minorités nationales, envoyant même dans les profondeurs de l'Asie des spécialistes pour codifier les traditions orales, le folk-lore, la langue même des peuples et rendre communicables les rêves et les pensées d'hommes avec qui les civilisés n'avaient cru devoir jusque-là entrer en communication autrement que pour les exploiter.

En ce temps où le dernier état indépendant d'Afrique est menacé par des pillards européens, où le beau ciel de France menace de se couvrir des avions de guerre de la répression césarienne, où tout ce que nous admirons et respectons en Allemagne, en Autriche et en Italie est en butte a la torture et à l'injure, où les colonies françaises sont, autant que jamais, traitées par des Français,non comme françaises mais comme colonies, nous n'avons pas oublié qu'une immense espérance a traversé la terre. Nous devons travailler avec nos amis du front populaire français, avec nos amis les communistes de l'Union Soviétique et de tous les pays, à supprimer le règne de la lâcheté financière et de la débilité mentale, particulièrement cléricale. Nous, écrivains antillais, sommes prêts à subordonner nos goûts personnels, artistiques et autres, les valeurs que notre édu-

Page two of L'Etudiant Noir, Volume 1, number 3 (May-June) *with an article by Leopold Sedar Senghor titled "Racisme? Non, mais Alliance spirituelle."*

LES IDÉES

Nègreries

Conscience Raciale et Révolution Sociale

Le matérialisme ne dit point que les pensées ne sont pas efficaces, mais seulement que leurs causes ne sont pas des pensées. Que leurs effets ne sont pas des pensées. (Nizan. Les Chiens de garde).

Quelle révolution fut jamais faite par le monde innocent des curiosités ? Qui souleva jamais un joujou contre son propriétaire? Pourtant, c'est bien là le tour de force que veulent entreprendre nos révolutionnaires nègres lorsqu'ils demandent au nègre de se révolter contre le capitalisme qui l'opprime. Le moyen, en effet d'appeler autrement qu'un joujou un peuple d'assimilés ? Dostoievsky le disait déjà, ou peu s'en faut : Toute race qui croit qu'elle n'a rien à dire au monde n'est qu'une « curiosité ethnique » et tout individu est un joujou qui croit qu'au rendez-vous du recevoir et du donner, son peuple arrive les mains vides.

« Agissez », dit-on au nègre. Mais comme agir c'est créer, et comme créer c'est pétrir et faire lever sa naturelle substance, le nègre [illegible] n'agira point, qui se distrait de [illegible] vit à part soi.

Un mal étrange nous ronge, en effet, aux Antilles : une peur de soi-même, une capitulation de l'être devant le paraître, une faiblesse qui pousse un peuple d'exploités à tourner le dos à sa nature, parce qu'une race d'exploiteurs lui en fait honte dans le perfide dessein d'abolir « la conscience propre des exploités ».

Les exploiteurs blancs nous ont donné, à nous autres exploités noirs, une culture, mais une culture blanche, une civilisation, mais une civilisation blanche, une morale, mais une morale blanche, nous paralysant ainsi par mailles invisibles pour le cas hypothétique où nous nous libérerions du plus sensible esclavage matériel qu'ils nous ont imposé. Et ils ourdissent leur trame, patiemment, inlassablement, par ruse diligente jusqu'à ce que nous mourions à la connaissance de nous-mêmes.

Dès lors, s'il est vrai, que le philosophe révolutionnaire est celui qui élabore les techniques de libération, s'il est vrai que l'œuvre de la dialectique révolutionnaire est de détruire « toutes les perceptions fausses prodiguées aux hommes pour voiler leur servitude », ne devons-nous pas dénoncer l'endormeuse culture identificatrice et placer sous les prisons qu'édifia pour nous le capitalisme blanc, chacune de nos valeurs raciales comme autant de bombes libératrices ? Ils ont donc oublié le principal ceux qui disent au nègre de se révolter sans lui faire prendre d'abord conscience de soi, sans lui dire qu'il est beau et bon et légitime d'être nègre.

Ils ont oublié de parler au nègre le seul langage qu'il puisse légitimement entendre, puisque, différent en cela de « l'employé du bureau de M. Gradgrind », « l'esclave nègre » a le sang riche encore d'affections humaines et que c'est d'une affection humaine, comme le fait remarquer Chesterton, qu'il aimera la fidélité ou la liberté.

La vérité est que ceux qui prêchent la révolte au nègre n'ont pas foi dans le nègre et que dans leur fierté d'être révolutionnai-

Above and continued on page 126: "Conscience Raciale et Revolution Sociale" by Césaire under the heading Les Idée and the sub-heading Négrerie.

res, ils oublient qu'ils sont nègres, premièrement et toujours : esclavage encore et de la plus stérile espèce.

Le héros de Paul Morand, « l'assimilé » Occide est révolutionnaire lui aussi : grâce à lui, Haïti a ses Soviets, Port-au-Prince devient Octobreville; bel avantage s'il reste prisonnier des blancs, singe stérilement imitateur !

Tant pis pour ceux qui se contentent d'être des Occide, par mépris de ce qu'ils appellent du « racisme ». Pour nous, nous voulons exploiter nos propres valeurs, connaître nos forces par personnelle expérience, creuser notre propre domaine racial, sûrs que nous sommes de rencontrer en profondeur, les sources jaillissantes de l'humain universel.

Ainsi donc, avant de faire la Révolution et pour faire la révolution, — la vraie —, la lame de fond destructrice et non l'ébranlement des surfaces, une condition est essentielle : rompre la mécanique identification des races, déchirer les superficielles valeurs, saisir en nous le nègre immédiat, planter notre négritude comme un bel arbre jusqu'à ce qu'il porte ses fruits les plus authentiques.

Alors seulement, nous aurons conscience de nous; alors seulement, nous saurons jusqu'où nous pouvons courir seuls ; alors seulement nous saurons où le souffle nous manque, et parce que nous aurons saisi notre particulière différence, et que nous « jouirons loyalement notre être », nous pourrons triompher de tous les esclavages, nés de la « civilisation ».

Etre révolutionnaire, c'est bien ; mais pour nous autres nègres, c'est insuffisant; nous ne devons pas être des révolutionnaires accidentellement noirs, mais proprement des nègres révolutionnaires, et il convient de mettre l'accent sur le substantif comme sur le qualificatif.

C'est pour cela qu'à ceux qui veulent être révolutionnaires uniquement pour pouvoir se moquer du nègre au nez « suffisamment

2

plati »; c'est pour cela qu'à ceux qui roient en Marx uniquement pour passer a ligne, nous disons :

Pour la Révolution, travaillons à prendre ossession de nous-mêmes, en dominant de aut, l'officielle culture blanche « gréement spirituel » de l'impérialisme conquérant.

Attelons-nous courageusement à la besogne culturelle, sans craindre de tomber dans n idéalisme bourgeois, l'idéaliste étant celui qui considère l'idée comme fille d'Idée t comme matrice d'idées, quand nous y oyons, nous, une promesse qui ne peut pas e pas s'épanouir en un buissonnement 'actes.

Oui, travaillons à être nègre, dans la certitude que c'est travailler pour la Révolution, car celui-là fera la Révolution qui sera dans sa force, et celui-là est dans sa force qui est dans son véritable caractère.

Aimé CESAIRE.

Continuation of "Conscience Raciale et Révolution Sociale" by Césaire on page two of L'Etudiant Noir, Volume 1, number 3 (May-June).

6 L'ETUDIANT NOIR

UN PEU DE POÉSIE ....

OBSESSION

par Léon DAMAS

Un goût de sang me vient,
me monte,
m'irrite le nez,
la gorge, les yeux.
Un goût de sang me vient,
m'emplit,
me baigne le nez,
la gorge, les yeux.
Un goût de sang me vient,
âcrement vertical pareil à
l'obsession païenne des encensoirs.

POUR SUR

par Léon DAMAS

Pour sûr j'en aurai
marre,
sans même attendre qu'elles prennent
les choses l'allure
d'un camembert bien fait.
alors je vous mettrai les pieds dans
le plat
ou bien tout simplement la main au collet
de tout ce qui m'emmerde
en gros caractères,
colonisation,
civilisation,
assimilation et la suite,
en attendant vous m'entendrez
souvent
claquer la porte.

[illegible]

MAINS NOIRES

par Richard WRIGHT

Je suis noir et j'ai vu des mains noires, des millions et des millions de mains noires.
Elles étaient fatiguées et gauches, et calleuses, et barbouillées, avec des ongles couverts d'envies
Elles étaient noueuses, écrasées, pressées,
Et elles frappaient sans trêve les machines palpitantes
Amassant des tas d'or de plus en plus volumineux sur les bancs des patrons,
Faisant des piles de plus en plus hautes d'acier,
De fer, de bois de charpente, de froment, de seigle, d'avoine,
De blé, de coton, de laine, de caisses d'huile, de charbon, de viande, de fruits, de verre,
Si bien qu'il y en eut plus qu'il n'en fallut.
Et les travailleurs noirs empoignèrent des fusils les mirent sur leurs épaules, marchèrent,
Occupèrent des tranchées, se battirent et tuèrent
Et vainquirent les nations
Qui achetaient les marchandises que les mains noires avaient fabriqué.
Et de nouveau, les mains noires amassèrent des tas de plus en plus volumineux de marchandises
Jusqu'à ce qu'il y en eût trop de nouveau.
Et les mains noires tombèrent oisives et se balancèrent sans travail,
Et devinrent molles et faibles et maigres, de chômage et de faim
Et elles devinrent nerveuses et elles se couvrirent de sueur, et elles s'ouvrirent et se fermèrent
[illegible]

[illegible]

LES HOMMES FORTS

par Sterling Brown

Ils vous ont arraché de votre terre natale,
Ils vous ont enchaîné en un troupeau d'esclaves,
Pêle-mêle, comme des cailles, ils vous ont entassé sur des ponts pleins d'ordure
Ils vous ont vendu pour enrichir une poignée de « Messieurs »

Ils vous ont dressé comme des bœufs,
Ils vous ont fouetté,
Ils vous ont marqué au fer rouge,
Ils ont fait de vos femmes des machines à faire des enfants,
Ils ont grossi votre nombre avec des bâtards...
Ils vous ont enseigné la religion qu'ils déshonoraient.

Vous chantiez :
Continuez à avancer d'un pouce
Comme un pauvre ver d'un pouce
Vous chantiez :
Tout à l'heure,
Je vais déposer ce pesant fardeau.
Vous chantiez :
Marchez ensemble, enfants
Ne soyez pas fatigués
Les hommes forts continuent d'avancer
Les hommes forts deviennent plus forts.

Ils montrent avec orgueil les routes que vous avez construites pour eux.
Ils roulent avec confort sur les rails que vous avez posés pour eux.
Ils vous mettaient des marteaux dans les mains
Et vous disaient : « Faites tant d'ouvrage avant la fin du jour »

[illegible]

Poetry on page 6 of L'Etudiant Noir, Volume 1, number 3 (May-June) *includes Cesaire's translation of Richard Wright's "Black Hands" and Damas's poetry.*

OBESSION

par Léon DAMAS.

Un goût de sang me vient,
me monte,
m'irrite le nez,
la gorge, les yeux.
Un goût de sang me vient,
m'emplit,
me baigne le nez,
la gorge, les yeux.
Un goût de sang me vient,
âcrement vertical pareil à
l'obsession païenne des encensoirs.

POUR SUR

par Léon DAMAS

Pour sûr j'en aurai
marre,
sansmême attendre qu'elles prennent
les choses l'allure
d'un camembert bien fait.
alors je vous mettrai les pieds dans
le plat
ou bien tout simplement la main au collet
de tout ce qui m'emmerde
en gros caractères,
colonisation,
civilisation,
assimilation et la suite,
en attendant vous m'entendrez
souvent
claquer la porte.

LIMBÉ (1)

par Léon DAMAS

Rendez-les moi mes poupées noires,
qu'elles dissipent
l'image des catins blêmes,
celle sempiternelle,
hallucinante,
noyés d'ombre,
de fantoches empilés fessus
dont le vent porte au nez la misère miséri-
[corde.
Donnez-moi l'illusion que je n'aurai à con-
[tenter
plus jamais
l'étale besoin des girouettes fardées mar-
[chands d'amour
des miséricordes allongées dévêtues ronflant
sous l'inconscient dédain du monde
et qui vont, viennent sur
le boulevard de mon ennui.
Rendez-les moi mes poupées noires que je joue
[avec elles
les jeux naïfs de mon instinct,
rester à l'ombre de ses lois,
recouvrer mon courage,
mon audace,
me sentir moi-même
à nouveau moi-même ce que hier j'étais
hier
sans complexité hier,
quand est venu l'heure du déracinement.
Ne sauront-ils jamais cette rancune de mon
[cœur,
à l'œil de ma méfiance ouvert trop tard,
ils ont cambriolé l'espace qui étaient miens,
la coutume, les jours; la vie,
la chanson, le rythme, l'effort,
le sentier, l'eau, la case,
la terre enfumée grise, la nuit, le ciel,
la sagesse, les mots, les
palabres, les
vieux,
la cadence, les mains, la mesure, les mains,
le piétinement, le sol.
Rendez-les moi mes poupées noires,
Mes poupées noires,
Poupées noires
Noires.

(1) Aux Antilles, nostalgie de l'être que l'on a perdu, par extension : spleen, cafard.

A closer view of Léon Damas's three poems, "Obsession," "Pour Sur," and "Limbé" published on page 6 of L'Etudiant Noir, Volume 1, number 3 (May-June).

As he echoed Locke anew, Césaire assigned the denotation of "Old Négritude" to elders and proclaimed the advent of the *Nouveau French Negro* in the following terms: "And in the midst of all that I say hurrah! My grandfather dies, I say hurray! The old négritude is progressively dying. Indeed, he was a good Negro."[10]

The term *negritude* was Césaire's own. Léon Damas, who was the first of the *Black Student* group to publish a book of poetry under the new banner of black cultural self-determination in the French empire, never used the term in any of his works. It is enlightening, in regard to Césaire's career, to recall that it was in opposition to the Martiniquan Communists' call to the West Indians to rise up under their banner that the term negritude was first expressed. Against this new trend for a West Indian "social revolution," Césaire proclaimed the primacy of racial consciousness and, in the process, used a word that in almost a century has been the subject of much debate.

Césaire and his views regarding the place of the Caribbean French colonies dominated the politics and the culture of the area for four generations. (Césaire was mayor of Fort de France, Martinique's capital city, and a deputy to France's General Assembly from 1945 until 2001. He retired at the age of eighty-eight.) His views also defined the political future of Guadeloupe, Martinique, and Guyane. It is, therefore, critical to understand his beliefs when he enunciated them for the first time.

Césaire begins his drive for the preeminence of negritude in *The Black Student* with a rhetorical question: "Who has ever roused a toy against its owner? For, is there another name for an assimilated people but a toy?"[11] Yet, it is to this "toy" that the West Indian Communists are calling to revolt. Devoid of any sense of themselves, such people are but an "ethnic curiosity" that arrive "empty handed at the cultural rendezvous."

To a people such as this, action is elusive because " ... acting is creating and since creating is to knead and make one's own natural substance rise, blacks who are diverted from themselves and live apart from themselves will never act." In subsequent paragraphs, Césaire draws the balance sheet of the process through which the West Indian lost his ability to act and became, concomitantly, a confirmed upholder of European cultural traits. Therefore, those who call on the West Indian to revolt in the name of dialectical materialism have forgotten to speak to him in the only language he can legitimately understand... The truth is that those who preach revolution to the West Indian have no faith in him and in their pride at being revolutionaries they have forgotten that they are black first and always. This is slavery of the most sterile nature.

To further underscore this point, Césaire uses the case of Haiti as viewed by Paul Morand in "The Black Tsar," a 1927 short story:

> Thanks to him (Morand's revolutionary hero, Occide, who fights against the American occupation) Haiti has its Soviets, Port-au-Prince becomes Octoberville. Where is the advantage if he [Occide] remains prisoner of the whites and a sterile imitating ape?

It is then, against the Occides of the world that Césaire brings about the second movement of his essay: "Too bad for those who, scorning what they call 'racism,' are content to be Occides. As for us, we want to exploit our own values, know our strengths through personal experience, dig our own racial domain..."

To Césaire, then, acceptance of these cultural and racial precepts is necessary before embarking upon the real revolution.

> Only then will we be conscious of ourselves; only then will we know how far we can run alone; only then will we know where we are lacking depth. Because we will have seized our particular difference and will completely possess our own self; we will then be in position to triumph over all slaveries born of 'civilization.'

Césaire, however, does not close the door completely to future cooperation with the Communists.

> It's fine to be a revolutionary; but for us blacks, it's not enough; we must not be revolutionaries who are accidentally black, but in fact black revolutionaries, and it is fitting, to put the accent on the substantive as well as on the qualitative ... For those who believe uniquely in Marx to cross the line, we say : For the Revolution, let us work at taking possession of ourselves, towering above, the official white culture of conquering imperialism ... Yes, let us work at being black, knowing that it is to work for the Revolution, because it is the one which will make the Revolution.

He concludes by reminding the black Marxists that to be at home is to be in one's "true character."

Negritude and Black Marxism

The tone and content of this essay in which Césaire goes armed with negritude into battle against the Marxist team of *Self Defense* are revealing. Within none of the passages is there mention of a time schedule or blueprint for an upcoming revolution based on the principles of negritude. Nor is there mention of a formula through which racial consciousness would flow from the initiated to the masses, thus inspiring a national culture based on the truism of negritude. Césaire does not advocate a dynamic negritude or adheres to any political concept to sustain a forthcoming national homeland, which would take root when negritude is triumphant. There is no room in Césaire's essay for any dialectical progression between the West Indian's future knowledge of his black self and a free homeland. In fact, Césaire does not entertain the inalienable right of West Indians under French rule to such a homeland devoid of a colonial supervisor in his criticism of the black Marxists.

The dichotomy between Césaire's "Racial Consciousness" in *The Black Student* and "Social Revolution" in *Self Defense* is, therefore, a faintly existent one, inasmuch as the latter does not prescribe either a program through which the victorious proletariat of the French West Indies would achieve nationhood. If anything, *Self Defense*'s goal is only slightly more general in tone and content than Césaire's, being in particular less ill defined. In fact, Césaire's disagreement with the group of *Self Defense* takes on the appearance of a family squabble in light of this comment from Césaire:

> There were two tendencies within our group. On the one hand, there were people from the Left, Communists at that time, such as J. Monnerot, E. Léro, and René Ménil. They were Communists, and therefore, we supported them. But very soon I had to reproach them—and perhaps I owe this to Senghor—for being French Communists. There was nothing to distinguish them either from the French Surrealists or from the French Communists.[12]

Césaire's call for racial consciousness, i.e., negritude, against the backdrop of the West Indian Communists' campaign for social revolution, is that neither ever envisaged proposing, at the time, that the big leap be made, that freedom from France be sought. The opposite is in fact true.

The objective of Césaire's call for the consciousness of one's "black self" in the French-speaking West Indies was, therefore, two-fold. One was the eradication of the old system of assimilation that had assumed and upheld the belief that since the black man was culturally hollow, Jacobin France's mission was to imbue him with French culture and mold him in its image. The above objective was essential to Césaire's aim of cultural and racial equality within the French nation; for assimilation intrinsically held the assimilated in a passive posture, and hence his inferior status. Assimilation, moreover, held him in economic and political bondage since "administrative Caesarism" was the economic and political arm of France's assimilationist grand design. The black communists, in their call for social revolution in the West Indies, having failed to address themselves to the dilemma of assimilation in a society hypothetically conscious of its racial differences would, if successful, in turn, maintain the cultural status quo. L. S. Senghor, in support of Césaire's thesis, asks: "After you have made the revolution what spiritual bread will you give to the black masses that you caused to lose its originality [further]?"[13] As in the past, they would continue to take their cue from Paris, not only on ideological matters but also on cultural ones. The socioeconomic stewardship of the colonies would be the only change. States Césaire,

> The white exploiters, gave us exploited blacks a culture, but a white culture; a civilization, but a white civilization; morality, but a white morality; thus paralyzing us with an invisible net in the hypothetical case we liberated ourselves from the most evident material slavery they imposed on us ... if it is true that the work of revolutionary dialectic is to destroy 'all false perceptions lavished on men to veil their state of servitude,' must we not denounce the paralyzing culture of identification ...

Césaire's second objective was the establishment of cultural self-determination for the French-speaking West Indies. This aim would remove the "assimilated" label from the Antilleans' vitae. In addition, it would bring about the institutionalization of an ethnic and cultural pluralistic French state within which the black Frenchman, having shed his former status would become—separately but equally—a full partner in the decisions made by the state on his behalf. In one movement in his *Return to my Native Land*, Césaire is found swearing by his negritude:

> I accept ...I accept ... totally, without reserve my race which no ablution
>
> of hyssop or mixed lilies could purify
>
> my race eaten by macula
>
> my race ripe grape for drunken feet I accept ... I accept ...[14]

The ensuing movement is the proclamation of his cultural autonomy, assimilation having been antithesized by his faith in negritude: Take me as I am. I am not adapting to you![15]

It is to fulfill this goal that he founded his own party in 1958. In his report to the Constitutional Assembly of the Progressive Party that he had founded, Césaire defined his political objective, as follows: "I say that the idea of federalism which is contrary to separation and at the same time contrary to assimilation is the only one which will correctly solve the West Indian problem."[16]

To Césaire, therefore, self-determination was a non sequitur; cooperation within what he called the "French family" based on the equality of the races and not the status quo assimilation of one race by another would be the logical derivative of black consciousness and the wave of the future. Like his student, Frantz Fanon, who had not yet made the vitiating leap out of alienation, questions and statements such as the following were neither unlikely nor out of order:

> What is all this talk of a black people, of a Negro nationality? I am a French man. I am interested in French culture, French civilization, the French people. We refuse to be considered "outsiders," we have full part in the French drama. When men who were not basically bad, only deluded, invaded France in order to subjugate her, my position as a Frenchman made it plain to me that my place was not outside but in the very heart of the problem. I am personally interested in the future of France, in French values, in the French nation, what have I to do with a black empire?[17]

The American experience had demonstrated to Césaire that expressions of black consciousness, such as the Negro Renaissance, were not antithetical to the blacks' goal of equal participation in the affairs of their country.

Chapter Seventeen
Pigment—Negritude in Revolt

Léon Damas published *Pigment* in 1937.[1] Had the Popular Front not been in power at the time, *Pigment* would not have been published that year.[2] In fact, it was seized in 1939, a few months following the fall of the Popular Front.

Besides the first few poems with surrealistic undertones,[3] *Pigment* is a conspicuously plain-spoken, revolutionary poetic project. Exile is its main inspiration—exile from Africa and exile from Guyane to France, where Damas's racial consciousness awoke and took shape in the fiery cry of *Pigment.* There is also the grievance against what colonial rule had made of Damas's homeland, detailed in *Return from Guyane* published one year later.

From exile to cultural alienation, Damas's moods shift constantly in *Pigment,* from humor to irony, from rancor to shame, all ending in revolutionary resolve. Damas's racial consciousness statements in purposeful verses are never compromising.

Pigment is read in the rhythm of jazz and blues inspired by Langston Hughes—uprooting, death, melancholy are expressed through a blood prism, while Damas never ceases, either forlornly or rancorously, to remind the listener of the degeneracy of his first exile. *Pigment* is also the ultimate aspiration of a New French Negro for Africa, for a way out of cultural alienation to arrive at a semblance of cultural self-determination.

Damas, concurrently with his "yearning to be black," reaches out for authenticity in dress and in behavior—an illustration of Freud's liberating influence from western civilization and decorum, promoted by the *Self Defense* group. Then, too, Damas never looses sight of the fact that only a minute interstice exists between one's consciousness and the actualization of that consciousness into revolt. And his awareness grows more and more acute as his frustrated feeling of revolt increases.

In one of the *Pigment* poems, "S.O.S.," Damas uses the coming of Fascism to shout his awareness and to warn that blacks in France are in mortal danger. ("S.O.S." was also the title of a poem by Etienne Léro in *Self Defense.*)

> Only then and not before will you all understand when they get the idea, and they'll get that idea soon, to go and stuff themselves on niggers like Hitler stuffing himself on Jews seven fascist days out of seven... and cutting off the sex of the blacks to make candles for their churches.[4]

The crescendo underlines the degradation of castration.

In the poem "On a Post Card," Damas preoccupation with the coming war is fraught with bitterness, recalling the number of blacks who have died for France; and the colonial habit of raising monuments to the dead following each of France's wars.[5]

"On a Post Card" and the next poem, "Et Caetera," assured that the French government would censor *Pigment*—Damas's call to revolt was too energetic; World War II too imminent. In these two poems, Damas summons blacks in the French colonies to direct their attention to the immediate problem of colonization and not to come to Europe to die for their colonizer.[6]

In Pigment's thirty-two poems, Damas hammered out in repetitive, sometimes abrupt and disjointed, rhythmic cadence, the balance sheet of the state of blacks under French rule. In the poem "On A Post Card," in particular, he attacked colonialism as a parasitic institution benefiting only the colonizers. In this instance, his countrymen would be used in a war they had no stake in, and only monuments would be raised to commemorate black lives given for the mother country.

Pigment devoid of any exoticism, does not only raise its jazz and blues voice against colonialism, it appeals to the blacks themselves "to leave" the assimilationist ways "in peace" and "to start by invading themselves and their homeland."

How was Damas judged at the time of *Pigment's* publication in 1937?

At Damas's funeral, forty-one years later, Césaire, the mayor of Fort de France, Martinique, in the vestibule of his City Hall, told the public:

> [Damas] was taken for a dreamer, a dotard, a sermonizer, a charlatan ... What strikes me is the seriousness in Damas, the tragedy in Damas, the pathos in Damas. Astonishing dignity for a man so many tended to take for a clown! When one really considers, it is not at all surprising – Damas was lucid to the highest degree. Truth can be cruel. The greatness of Damas is to accept it, without altering it, without erasing it, without embellishing it. As there is the Sartrian nausea, there is fundamentally the Damasian hiccup which is disgust, repulsion, attempts never completely fulfilled because it is loaded with impossibilities of rejection and expulsion.[7]

Undertaken in behalf of the Paris Ethnographic Museum, Damas's next work, *Return from Guyane (Retour de Guyane),* is a documentary on the conditions of his homeland. Due to its unyielding criticism of French colonial policies, *Return from Guyane* would not have been published in 1938 had the Popular Front not been in power.

In this exposé, Damas denounces the "trash heap" character French various colonization schemes had given Guyane. Like many European powers in one or several areas of the Third World, the French had chosen New Caledonia and then Guyane as its rubbish chute for criminals of all sorts, not only to remove them from France's streets, but also to consolidate colonization.

At their apartment in southwest Washington, DC, circa 1975, Leon Gontran Damas with his wife Marietta Campos. Between them is their friend, Louise-Anne Monlouis-Eugénie. Damas was a distinguished professor at Howard University's African Studies Department from 1974 until his death in 1978. Unlike his beloved friend Césaire, Damas was not an intellectual; nevertheless, he made the most—especially in the United States—of being one of the "Founders of the Negritude Movement" on the same line as the illustrious Leopold S. Senghor and Aimé Césaire. Un écorché vif, he expressed himself best in his poems. Césaire looked on him as the father of modern black Francophone poetry. Damas said that poetry was an art form Senghor did not possess, considering that in his words, "Senghor wrote poetry with the help of a French dictionary." The author's novel, The Beggars' Pursuit, *follows the negritude proponents' activities in Paris, circa 1936*

Due to the difficulties of escape inherent in Guyane's geography, convicts walks unguarded the streets of the capital, Cayenne. "[The prisoner]," reports Damas, "roams the streets, terrorizes, rapes our children, implants his mores in the society, debases it, corrupts it, automatically depraves it; he is an outlaw that hunger and needs make dangerous."[8] Penitentiary officials use the criminals as laborers and domestics, a practice that has a degenerative impact on Guianese society.

In *Return from Guyane,* Damas's outrage echoes the revolt in *Pigment,* enunciating the centuries of Guianese deprivation from French colonial rule. For example, the lepers of Acarouany, in the interior, exist in an appalling state; for, except in the capital city, basic medical facilities were non-existent in 1938. The rich Guianese soil is left to the jungle, and industry of any kind—except for the penal colony—is absent from the territory. "Guyane," Damas reports, "is the most wretched French colony in the richest territory in the world."[9]

On assimilation, Damas affirms in the chapter "For or Against Assimilation," that France's efforts to make white Frenchmen of Guianese is futile. Taking Leopold S. Senghor as an example, he affirms that although his friend, thanks to France, has become an "eminent specialist in the French language . . . why would [France] at this price want [Senghor] to abandon his Serere quality [his *Négritude*] admitting that he could."[10] On the issue of *departmentalization*—incorporation—of the "old colonies," he reviews the conditions of the school system in Guyane, the state of transportation, the abuse of power by French officials, and concludes that without any significant change in its socioeconomic infrastructure Guyane would become a French department in name only. It would still be France's "garbage disposal." [Departmentalization] will not lessen the disgust which the American, the Brazilian, the Englishman, the Dutch experience when they stop in Guyane."[11] He also warns France that the United States, which has the capability to develop Guyane, is expressing interest in its annexation. Both France and the colonies used the United States as boogeyman to frighten each other. France pointing at the living condition of blacks in the U.S.; the colonies at the likelihood that America would provide more for them.

Return from Guyane is a thesis against France's colonial policies. It is in prose the demonstration of the racial and political consciousness of the "New 'French' Negro" that *Pigment* is in verse. Both *Pigment* and *Return from Guyane* claim cultural self-determination for the French colonies. Unlike others who insisted on complete assimilation within French culture, Damas and his colleagues from *The Black Student* argue for an equality of cultures whereby—hypothetically—a black Frenchman does not have to become alienated in order to belong to a French community of diverse nations. Damas argues that the colonized can be equal to the French and still retain his own identity.[12] Damas ends his prophetic[13] documentary by proposing that Guyane's vast gold deposits be mined to serve the colony.

Mine de Rien is introduced here in the context of *Return from Guyane*. It is, at the time of this writing, Damas's unpublished collection of thirty-six poems, completed just prior to his death in January 1978. It evokes the gold mines of his youth. *Mine*—(gold) mine—is a play on the word *mine*, appearance. (When Damas read these poems with the author, the latter understood *Mine* to mean "gold mine.") *Mine de Rien* in this case would be translated as *Mine of Nothing*, Damas being keenly aware at the time of his death that Guyane was still a mine of nothing. This explains *Mine de Rien*'s bitter reminiscences and resentment, all derived from the awareness that Damas had not been able to change the status of his homeland. So keen was Damas's sensitivity that it would not be wrong to call him *un écorché vif.*

Mine de Rien contains few of the youthful *engagé* poetry found in *Pigment*. Damas has replaced virulent denunciation against colonial policies toward his homeland with a morose, regretful lament. The first poem in the collection, "Mine de Riens," is an example:

Mine of nothing   Mine de rien

wealthy   riches

from the only sap   des seuls seve

sugar   suc

salt from the hard earth   sel de la terre ferme

Afro-Amérindian   aframérindienne

mine   mienne

seeded   ensemencée

watered   abreuvée

fed   nourrie

from the blood   du sang

from the sweat   de la sueur

of my offered pain— de ma peine offerte—

not without pain non sans peine

so that all pour que tout

could be pour que fût

so that all can be. pour que tout soit.[14]

M I N E D E R I E N S

Poèmes inedits , par Leon G. DAMAS

Mine de Riens	
N'Attendez	
A Croupetons dans la Nuit	(2 pags)
Sauvage-de-Bons-Sens	(3 "
A La Rubrique Des Cheins Creves	5 "
Point Trop N'En Faut	4 "
Excusez du Peu	2 "
Au Banquet de Cloture	
Passe Encore	2 "
Je Le Confesse Mon Reverend	2 "
Parce qu'Elle Avait Eu Pour Pere	
On m'Ecrit	
Je Dis	
Qu'en Savent-ils	
Non le Vent	
M'Est Avis	
Seuls Ceux qui Disent	
Et Pourquoi	
Il me revient	2 "
Elles	
Elle Avait dans le Regard	
Autant Elle Avait	
Au Bout du Fil	3 "
Sur Un Tableau de Max Ernst	
S'Il Faut En Croire	
Il N'Y Avait Pas Que La Grisaille	
Me Revient	
Chose Promise	
Autant Le Voir En Cage	
Poursuivant son Reve	
De Qui	
Pour Peu	
Nous n'Irons plus	
Puisque	8 "
De la Profuse et diffuse Cleur Fauve	4 "
A D'Autres	

The author read the Mine de Rien *poems with Léon Damas about a year before Damas's death. Damas would make corrections as seen above and on the opposite page, and his wife, Marietta Campos, would type a clean copy.*

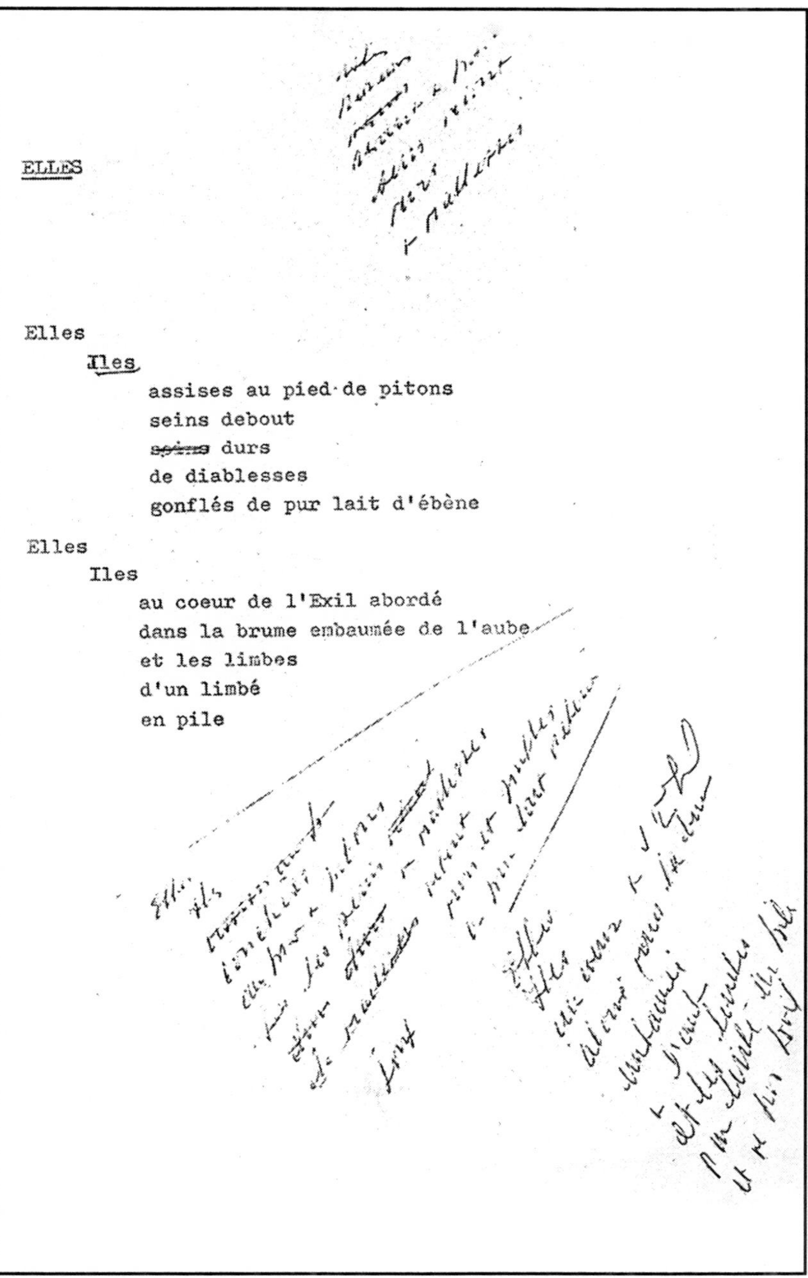

ELLES

Elles
    Iles
        assises au pied de pitons
        seins debout
        ~~seins~~ durs
        de diablesses
        gonflés de pur lait d'ébène

Elles
    Iles
        au coeur de l'Exil abordé
        dans la brume embaumée de l'aube
        et les limbes
        d'un limbé
        en pile

Chapter Eighteen
Césaire, Negritude, and Politics in the French West Indies

Césaire returned to Martinique, in August 1939, already a legend in French academic circles for his deft intellect and ability to wield the French language with singular dexterity.[1] It was, however, the heralding of his negritude that set him apart from the other returning students who had all traveled to Paris to continue their studies to take their place in the colonial system. Frantz Fanon who two years later entered Césaire's literature class at the local secondary school, recalled that:

> For the first time a secondary school teacher – a man, therefore, who was apparently worthy of respect—was seen to announce quite simply to (Martiniquan society) 'that it was fine and good to be a Negro' …what indeed could be more grotesque than an educated man, a man with a diploma, having in consequence understood a good many things, among others that it was unfortunate to be a Negro, proclaiming that his skin was beautiful and that the 'big black hole' was a source of truth … He must be mad, for it was unthinkable that he could be right.[2]

Before his return and during the period he milited from his Paris base against the communists' principles of *Self Defense*, Césaire outlined his role in the new Martinique, in *Return to My Native Land.* Here he measures his determination to become the leader who will extirpate Martinique from its paralyzing colonial inertia:

> I will come back to this country of mine
>
> and I will say to it : 'Embrace me without fear. If all I can do is
>
> speak, it is for you that I will speak.
>
> My mouth will be the mouth of the misfortunes that have no
>
> Mouth; my voice the liberty
>
> of those who are stuck in the dungeon of despair.[3]

Césaire's plan remained shelved for six years. On his way home war was declared in Europe. In the French West Indies, a Pétain lieutenant, Admiral Georges Robert, with the help of "ten thousand" French sailors imposed Vichy's will on the area from 1939 to 1943.[4] This period witnessed the crystallization of the aspirations of the people of Martinique to solidify their amalgamation into France, and Césaire's appreciation of the black masses as a class.

The presence of French sailors overtly displaying their fascist tendencies produced in the black population of Martinique the breakdown of the ironic mechanism, which until then had shielded them from the recognition of their "dark skinned self."[5]

> In 1939 no [Antillean] in [the West Indies] proclaimed himself to be a Negro, claimed to be a Negro. When he did, it was always in his relations with a white man. It was the white man, the 'bad white man,' who obliged him to assert his color, more exactly to defend it ...[6]

The difference between the real and the mythical France conceived by an anxious people—continuously in search of one more defense against the reality of the French West Indies—is central to the understanding of the motivations there.

> By a process easy to understand the West Indian had perceived France of the sailors into the bad France, and the Marseillaise that those men respected was not their own. Those sailors were racists. Now, everybody knows that the true Frenchman is not a racist; in other words, he does not consider the West Indian a Negro. Since these men did so consider him, this meant that they were not true Frenchmen.[7]

In June 1943, the Martiniquan masses later supported by the army of which three-fourths were from the island, overthrew the Vichy regime there. This was done not in the name of negrohood as Fanon suggests, but in the name of the mythical France which de Gaulle (who had opposed Pétain) came to symbolize. Like Schoelcher and the Jacobins of 1794, de Gaulle proclaimed "liberty, equality, fraternity" and gained god-like appeal and unmatched veneration in the French West Indies. He had, by opposing the forces, which Pétain and Robert upheld, become the answer to the question about the future of the West Indies within the French empire. The political course was thus set.

The Vichy experience had deepened the fears that France could renounce Guyane and the West Indies islands. Such apprehension contributed to demands for irrevocable bonds between the mother country and the colonies. Any political party supporting such demands would have carried the day at the elections that took place after the war. And the communists were the most uncompromising in the advocacy of those demands. Since they had also emerged from the war as the dominant party in France, they were most instrumental in bringing them to fruition.

"It is logical [then] that the elections that followed the Liberation should have delegated two communist deputies out of three."[8] It only helped that Césaire, following the trend, had, in the meantime, joined them.

In Martinique in 1941, Césaire founded and was director of a new periodical, *Tropiques*. His collaborator, René Ménil of the old *Self Defense* team, gave this periodical its orientation and temper. *Tropiques*, to a fundamental extent, projected more of the ideologies *Self Defense* had stood for than the "racial consciousness" propounded by Césaire in *The Black Student*. Beginning with the first two issues, Menil sets the poetic orientation of the periodical with articles such as "Birth of Our Act" and "Poetic Orientation." Césaire who hosted surrealist guru, André Breton in 1941, and who had discovered that surrealism greatly enhanced his ability to dwell into his "dark skinned self," began in turn to publish in *Tropiques's* third issue, poems with definite surrealist bents. Césaire's political perception of the Martiniquan masses had also been extended to include the views that *Self Defense* had expounded earlier. Whereas he had previously upheld negritude as the sine qua non driving force of change, in wake of the overthrow of the Robert-led Vichy regime, he began to associate consciousness of race with consciousness of class. In his "Toussaint L'Ouverture," for example, Césaire writes : "This class of black peasants matured by events was for now a 'class by itself' … and no more a 'class in itself.' Determined to finish with a tired social order, it could not accept that this order continue under the guise of race privilege or of caste."[9] The black masses of the French West Indies thus became for Césaire the proletariat, and the descendants of the slave owners who had also sided with the fascists became "the tired order" to be overthrown. By 1944, Menil could, therefore, say of Césaire in the eleventh issue of *Tropiques*:

> Conceived in 1932 in *Self Defense*, this cultural movement of the French West Indian people was launched effectively only in 1940 … It was constantly oriented by sure technical means derived from human sciences such as psychoanalysis, historical materialism, ethnography. The master conductor of this movement was Aimé Césaire.[10]

(Ménil who continued to perceive negritude as a 'reactionary doctrine,' granted Césaire's *Black Student* only ethnography in his acknowledgement of contributors to the French West Indian cultural movement).[11]

Nine years after he had defined his role in "racial consciousness" terms in response to *Self Defense*'s call to "social revolution," Césaire had incorporated enough of the latter's precepts to have, like *Tropiques*, become the synthesis of the two interwar movements of the West Indian students in Paris.

Recognized by Ménil and others with the same artistic and political convictions as their leader, Césaire had now achieved the goal he had set for himself in *Return to My Native Land*. It is axiomatic that had he already made his mark in Martinique by 1945, Césaire would certainly have founded a party reflecting his Negritude-Marxist views then and not wait until March 1958. It follows that, although he was closer ideologically to the Communist Party, (C.P.) than any other, his choice of the C.P. for his ticket, when he became a candidate for political office was an opportunistic, albeit a logical, one. Susan Frutkin, commenting on Césaire's participation in the Communist Party, explains:

> For practical purposes, the Communist Party of Martinique, as an arm of the French Communist Party, offered badly-needed support and experience as well as a vehicle to national political power for these new political leaders. This was of considerable importance for those who believed that solutions to the island's problems might come from above, from a government which had the interest of the working class and possibly the black colonials at heart.[12]

It is not coincidental that Césaire's disenchantment with the Party followed the general decline of the left's popularity in both France and Martinique and the rise of his own at home. His letter of resignation from the C.P. to Maurice Thorez is, moreover, reflective of the views he elaborated in *The Black Student* in 1935, and is symptomatic of the "accent on the substantive as well as on the qualitative" which he consistently emphasized.

His advocation of cultural and political autonomy—negritude—within a French federal state, could only have suffered when Césaire became a member of a party that mirrored so closely the centralism innate to France's political order. Admittedly, negritude was 'put on ice' during the time Césaire remained in the French Communist Party. However, the C.P. offered the West Indian masses, while in power, the guarantee of a French umbrella, which is precisely the leitmotif in Césaire's enunciation of negritude.

Conclusion

The assimilation of African descendants in Guadeloupe, Guyane, Martinique and St. Domingue began before the 1789 French Revolution had decreed these territories integral parts of the mother country. The 1685 *Le Code Noir*, for example, proposed to give a semblance of legal protection to the slave against his master. Because the Code came from Paris, it was a conspicuous measure by which Black people could judge France in relation to their immediate masters in the colonies. The Revolution was, however, the main factor in the French assimilation drive of these "Old Colonies." With its enunciation of the "Rights of Man and the Citizen," which applied also to the blacks, the France of 1789 became the beacon which guided the African descendant in the belief that assimilation was deliverance.

It was precisely to consolidate the work of the revolution with respect to colonial matters that Toussaint L'Ouverture drafted the first constitution since the "Code Noir" in St. Domingue to make his government Paris's partner in the exploitation of France's richest colony. Napoleon's re-enslavement scheme, however, unleashed the desperate drive for freedom in both Guadeloupe and St. Domingue. Pélage's trust in France doomed Guadeloupe's chances for self-rule in 1802. As a result, slavery was re-imposed there. In St. Domingue, on the other hand, owing in part to the great number of uncreolized Africans taking part in the revolution, freedom was maintained and independence proclaimed in 1804.

The French-educated people of color in Haiti who replaced the white Creoles in the elite position maintained a bias toward French culture. They built a social, cultural, and economic barrier between themselves and the Afro-Haitian peasantry as well as the other elite, the military. Devoid of any genuine national perspective, neither the educated elite nor the army was up to the task of providing the necessary leadership in the hostile Western Hemisphere and against France and the planters' lobby determined on compensation for the loss of their slaves. Consequently, Haiti in 1915, fell prey to an American occupation, which lasted nineteen years.

In the other French colonies, blacks and people of color looked toward the France of the Jacobins to support their efforts to abolish slavery and to acquire French citizenship in their struggle against the ruling class of white Creoles. They believed that, through amalgamation and complete assimilation of the colonies, the power and wealth of the Creoles would be re-apportioned and French citizenship opportunities would be accessible in the West Indies and Guyane. Concurrently, there evolved a culture whose literature was a by-product of the efforts toward the cultural and political assimilation of the colonies. Haitian writers during the same period had for goal the recognition of their country as a "civilized" (read French-speaking) albeit independent nation. Although largely reflective of the French, Haitian literature was much more fertile, its writers more inventive than writers from the remnant French colonies. Haitian writers, then, in the second half of the nineteenth century, began to write extensively of their preoccupation with the ominous direction their country was taking. A number of them also became preoccupied with the idea of an independent Haiti rehabilitating the black race. In the French colonies, such contemplation did not take place in view of the fact that no one accepted and articulated the goal of an independent Guyane or French-speaking West Indies. On the contrary, the West Indian and Guianese writers created an exotic French regionalization of literature in their further attempts to make their colonies provinces of France. They succeeded. In the 1970s Guadeloupe, Guyane, and Martinique became French regions, above the departmental status, which they had achieved on March 19, 1946.

Literature, if a wide window on society, is not, however, the only criterion by which to judge peoples' aspirations. In Haiti, for example, the peasant, who lived much as his ancestors had done in Benin or Guinea, maintained a genuine, sustaining culture to battle the elements that nature and his country's elites imposed upon him. When the Marines landed and once again the fear of slavery loomed large, it was the Afro-Haitian Cacos who took to the hills to resist. The elite who had driven the country into bankruptcy turned to them, at Price-Mars' urging, for cultural authenticity to counter the occupation. A social and racial revolution followed the drive for accuracy by the Haitian literati. Men such as Dumarsais Estimé, who had militated for the Haitianization of the elite's culture and literature, were elected to the presidency following the American occupation.

Estimé undertook to revolutionize Haiti's society as Price-Mars had done in literature. For the first time the Afro-Haitian received some benefits from his government. Haiti's 'old man discord,' however, re-imposed himself and the elites resumed their fratricidal conflicts until the presidency for life of Francois Duvalier put an end to the dissension.

The thoughts of Jacques Roumain, the preeminent writer-intellectual of that period, did not germinate in Haiti. The Afro-Haitians, to whose betterment Roumain dedicated his literary talent and his later years, still lived in stagnation. In October 1937, for example, Dominican dictator Rafael Trujillo's forces murdered more than twenty thousand Haitian migrant workers in St. Domingue. It seems that the intellectual vitality, the nationalism, and the newly acquired knowledge that all Haitians shared a common cultural heritage, which the American Occupation and Price-Mars had awakened in the elite, never took place. It's like Jacques Roumain never was; nothing changed in Haiti. Moreover, many of the writers, who wrote to counter the occupation as well as those who politically tried to revamp Haitian society, took residence abroad. A number also were killed. Price-Mars, thirty-nine years after the publication of the epoch-making *Thus Spoke the Uncle*, lamented:

> ... I recognize that I was wrong to think that fifteen years of foreign occupation had chased away the old man who lies in each of us; that the interference of the American army in our affairs had been enough to humiliate those among us who aspired to take back the reins with a more sober sense of justice, of freedom and social progress.[1]

The literary creation that emanated from the demand for social and cultural uplift at the time of the occupation was for the consumption of the educated elite only. In spite of the Haitian literary fecundity, eighty percent of the Haitian people remain illiterate and never read any of the oeuvres the occupation incited the few who could read and write to produce. Masses and elite were no more than strangers from different worlds.

In France, following the First World War, black Americans, Africans of the French empire, and a number of West Indians and Guianese influenced each other into enunciating and claiming their "dark-skinned selves." In the case of the West Indians and the Guianese, five names stand out. René Maran, whose novel *Batouala* opened the flow of criticism of France's colonial policies in Africa; Paulette Nardal, who co-founded the first bilingual West Indian periodical dedicated to racial assertion and cooperation between blacks in Paris; Etienne Léro, who founded the periodical *Self Defense* and who gave French West Indian literature its surrealist and communist tint; Aimé Césaire, who, together with Léon G. Damas, Leopold S. Senghor and others, founded the periodical *The Black Student* and spoke of negritude; Léon Damas, who was the first of these writers to declare the negritude of people under French rule in the collection of poems, *Pigment*, and a documentary, *Return from Guyane*, on the conditions of his homeland.

Again, unlike the Haitian writers whose majority was involved in the Haitianization of culture and literature by the end of the American Occupation in 1934, the majority of French West Indians and Guianese literati still produced French regionalized works also at the time when the *The Black Student* group led by Césaire made negritude known in 1935.

The mathematics of the colonial situation in the French-speaking West Indies in 1946, in relationship to Césaire's enunciation of negritude are known. What are the conclusions? The negritude propounded by Césaire was aimed at providing to the assimilated French-speaking West Indian a disalienating option at the cultural level and concomitantly establish in the political arena a French federation whereby the West Indian, divested of his subordinated self, would become a partner of Paris. The call for the transformation of a unitarian French republic into a federal commonwealth by both Césaire and Senghor was at heart a quixotic attempt to salvage a world where the distinctness of black French-speaking men was possible in a universal French nation. The method, which France used to disarm on the one hand Senghor's demands and on the other Césaire's, demonstrates the unilateralness of the decision-making system in force between mother country and colony.

In the case of Senghor, the establishment of a political structure already making provisions for the fragmentation of France's Equatorial and West African colonies accompanied the enactment on June 23, 1956, of the Loi Cadre (the colonial administrative decentralizing law). Consequently, in spite of Senghor's affirmation that "the peoples of Africa do not intend to cut themselves off from metropolitan France; they want to be able to construct side by side with her their own edifice, which will consolidate and extend French territory,"[2] de Gaulle was set upon dismemberment of France's African empire, thus, tolling the death knell for Senghor's dream of a federal French commonwealth. According to de Gaulle's minister of information, Alain Peyrefite, de Gaulle said,

> It's well and good that there be Yellow Frenchmen, Black Frenchmen, and Brown Frenchmen. It shows that France is opened to all races and has a vocation for the universal. However, they must remain a small minority. Otherwise, France would no longer be France. We are after all a European people, of the white race, of Greek and Latin culture and of the Christian religion.[3]

In the case of Césaire, it was simpler for de Gaulle to disregard Césaire's aspiration. For, whereas, Senghor's ambition was also victimized by African nationalists like Guinea's Ahmed Sékou Touré, Césaire's gamble that

Senghor would include "the overseas provinces in a possible federal system,"[4] was side-lined by events which led to the formation of the short-lived French Community (Communauté) followed by independence for the African colonies. But Senghor's personal commitment toward France, together with his conviction that the colonies could not go it alone without Paris's assistance, were such that his elaborate negritude prescription served to maintain a neo-French colonial status over Dakar long after Senegal had gained *de jure* independence.[5]

France dismissed Césaire's effort to redeem the autonomy package of his ill-fated federal dream with de Gaulle's March 16, 1964, one-liner—the West Indies are not Africa which has the geographical mass and a culture of its own to be independent—the West Indies, without France's protection, are only specks in the ocean between Europe and the Americas at any one's (read the United States') mercy.[6]

The fallacies in Césaire's formulae have their roots in the reality that the colonizer has the inherent right of first approval—that it is up to France to acknowledge and recognize Césaire as a new black French man mutated from the "old négritude." If France recognizes that a partnership between the mother country and the colonies is in its interest, it may then give its consent. The one-sidedness of the colonial *l'Exclusif* remains in force; the mother country is still making the decisions for the colonies.

An example of colonial exclusivity in the latter part of the twentieth century occurred when, starting in 1963, the mother country decided to sponsor immigration to France from its oldest colonies: Guyane, Guadeloupe, Martinique and Reunion. Through the BUMIDOM (Bureau pour le développement des migrations dans les départements d'outre-mer – Office for immigration expansion in overseas provinces), the program's goal was to provide cheap labor to France's post-World War II expanding economy and concomitantly diffuse unemployment and public restlessness in the "overseas provinces" during the independence-granting period in Africa and the end of the successful Algerian Revolution. As people moved from the "ex" colonies to the mother country, people from the mother country moved to the "former" colonies.[7] In 1978, Césaire reacted to this transfer of people, calling it "génocide par substitution"[8] —genocide through substitution. Césaire did not go beyond making a memory-catching pronouncement regarding a program that further consolidated France's oversight of Guyane, Guadeloupe, and Martinique.

It is true that Césaire's enunciation of negritude was an emancipatory act. However, because it lacked a freedom from France component, paradoxically as the post-World War II national liberation surge was about to begin in earnest in Africa and Asia, Césaire's negritude was but one more adjustment the descendants of the captive Africans in the French-speaking West Indies and Guyane have made since abolition to remain bound to the mother country. The result is that Césaire's call for "racial consciousness" remained a limp force, lacking the dynamic element that would thrust it into the colonial realities of the marginal French West Indies. In Césaire's attempts to develop a common ground on which negritude could strive within a dependent French entity, Césaire had not paid heed to the fact that "in the colonial situation, culture, deprived of the double support of the nation and the state, withers and agonizes. The condition of cultural existence is, therefore, national liberation."[9] The inherent promise of freedom that negritude proclaimed was stifled, therefore. For "independence [the nation-state] ... is an indispensable condition for the existence of men and women who are truly liberated, in other words who are truly masters of all the material means which make possible the radical transformation of society."[10]

In comparing both Haitian nationalism, Haitianism, and Negritude, it is clear that the first evolved from a higher stage of cultural and political consciousness than the latter. Whereas, for example, at the end of the nineteenth century a number of Haitian writers, such as Antenor Firmin, were already defending their race and its contribution to civilizations, writers of the French West Indies and Guyane still considered the "racial question" a subject not to be written about. *Haitianism*, clearly, had a better chance of sustaining the elite in Haiti in the drive for authenticity than negritude had in the French West Indies and Guyane.

As a rule, the centuries of interracial unions and colonization have added an undeniably strong European factor to the culture of the French West Indies and Guyane, which the concept of negritude espoused by Aimé Césaire does not fully evoke. Consequently, a concept much like Haitianism has evolved from negritude that attempts to come to grips with the cultural and racial amalgamation that has taken place in the French West Indies and Guyane over the centuries of colonization. This idea is *Antillanity*, first given credence by Gilbert Gratiant of Martinique, in response to Etienne Léro's bitter criticism, in *Self Defense*, of Gratiant's book of poems, *Poems in False Verses*. Of this work, Lero said, "Gratiant's verses translate neither the social inequities of his country nor the passion of his race."[11] In 1948 Gratiant responded to Lero's censure with a long poem, *Credo of the Mixed Bloods*, or *I Want To Sing of France*, to defend his belief in the qualities and values inherent in the interchange between Africa and Europe in the West Indies and Guyane. In 1981 Edouard Glissant conceptualized Antillanity, to assert the cultural and racial reality particular to the French West Indies and Guyane. In 1989, three writers from Martinique, Patrick Chamoiseau, Raphaël Confiant and Jean Bernabé called for a *Créolité* movement that would break the monopoly of French and promote the Creole language in the literature of Guadeloupe, Guyane, and Martinique.

Negritude is not, however, an anachronistic precept to the French West Indies' and Guyane's current social, cultural, and political realities. On the contrary, in nations where the fear of going it alone, shorn of the French guardian, is the leitmotif of every day life, Antillanity, Créolité, etc., have no value, unless the basic consciousness of one's negritude takes place.

But, the dilemma of Césaire's negritude remains the dilemma of the French West Indies and Guyane: a concept in search of a rooting soil, a rooting soil in quest of an identity.

Appendix
Interview with Josie Fanon, Frantz Fanon's Widow

After six years of revolutionary activities in Africa, Frantz Fanon arrived in New York in early October 1961, suffering from an advanced case of leukemia. Admitted to Bethesda Naval Hospital, he died on December 6th. He was thirty-six years old.

Born in Martinique in 1925, Fanon was a product of the colonial system discussed above. In 1944, he joined the Free French forces to help protect "true France" against the racist French sailors stationed in Martinique during the war—those "sailors who had forced [him] to defend and thus discover [his] color."

The army experience sharpened his awareness of the world where division and racism were the rule. His experience and a keen, sensitive mind made him one of the most lucid observers of the realities inherent to colonialism.

Until the Algerian Revolution, Fanon adhered to the principles of Negritude espoused by Aimé Césaire, his lycée teacher. *Black Skin White Mask* is a Negritude testimonial in which Fanon acknowledges blackness albeit from the point of view of his French colonial upbringing and Césaire's adaptation concerning the place of peoples of African descent in the French empire, discussed above.

His uncompromising efforts on behalf of the Algerian Revolution shortened his life, while giving him unparalleled insight into and appreciation for national liberations and struggles found in his writing. Today, we speak of a Fanon legacy.

Fanon's wife, Josie, came to the United States and visited the author at Howard University. In this short interview, she gives a glimpse into the life and views of her husband, author of *The Wretched of the Earth*.

The interview of Mme Josie Fanon took place on November 16, 1978, at Howard University's African-American Center. Josie Fanon committed suicide at El Biar, Algiers, ten years later. Born Marie-Joseph Dublé in Lyon, France, she was 58 years old.

CF: What are the reasons for your visit to the United States this year?

J.Fanon: I came back this year because of an invitation from the United

Nations Special Committee Against Apartheid, which is organizing throughout the year a series of homage and commemorations to black revolutionaries, notably Paul Robeson, Nelson Mandela of the A.N.C., President Nkrumah, etc. It is in this context that the committee decided to pay tribute to Frantz and invited me.

CF how do you feel about this second trip to the United States?

J.Fanon: From a personal point of view, I am a bit shaken to be back in the U.S. because it is where my husband died. I am also interested in observing the black civil rights movements in the US, examine the new perspectives and discuss what the hopes are.

CF: You were in the U S previously in 1961. When exactly in 1961 were you here and what were your reasons fro that trip?

J.Fanon: I came to the United States in November 1961 because my husband was hospitalized at the NIH Bethesda Hospital. The Algerian Provisional Government (APG) had sent him here for medical care. One year earlier, while representing the provisional government in Ghana, doctors diagnosed him with leukemia. They first sent him to Moscow for treatment, but the disease worsened; and the APG, with the Tunisian government's assistance, asked the Americans for help.

At the time, they believed that the best medical facilities were in the United States. It was under these circumstances that he came to the U.S.

However, you should note that he did not come here of his own accord. In fact, he was not in favor of this solution. As a black man, a militant, and an anti-imperialist revolutionary fighter, he was not comfortable going to the United States. But really, he had no choice. He was very ill—in fact, he was dying.

CF: You were telling me when we passed through the campus gate, that your son, Olivier, had spent some time at Howard University in 1961. Would you say more about that?

J.Fanon: My son was a toddler at the time and because I had to take care of my husband—I was here more than a month—I visited Frantz everyday and spent many nights at the hospital with him. During that time, we enrolled our small son at Howard University's kindergarten.

CF what is your occupation today?

J.Fanon: I have been for sometime a professional journalist. I worked from 1962—the year of Algeria's independence—until last year [1977] for the Algerian press. I also worked with the Algerian Front for National Liberation in the information section. Since 1977, I have worked for a Pan-African magazine, *Demain L'afrique* (*Tomorrow Africa*) published monthly in Paris. That's the reason I live in Paris now.

CF: How did you meet Frantz Fanon?

J.Fanon: I met him in Lyon (in the southeast of France). We were both students. He was in medical school; I was in liberal arts. We met at a theatre. He was 23; I was 18.

CF: Speaking of Lyon, would you retrace for us the course of Fanon's life?

J.Fanon: When I met Frantz, he had been already in France about four years. Understand that he was from Martinique; born in a French colony, he had assimilated all the cultural values of France. This pathology is common to the people of the French-speaking Antilles. Even today, these colonies are the territories where French colonialism has been the most over-emphasized, most perfidious, and most noxious.

In the first stage of Frantz's life, while still very young, he joined the Free French Forces during the Second World War. This meant that for a time, he identified with France. However, when he went to France and confronted French society's racism, he began to understand and he analyzed his personal and his countrymen's experiences. The result of this analysis is in *Black Skin, White Mask* published in 1952. He was twenty-five at the time.

During that time, he was also a medical student, specializing in psychiatry. At the completion of his studies, he wanted to go back to the Antilles or to Africa to look for work. For administrative reasons, he was unable to get a position in Martinique, Guadeloupe, or Senegal; so he picked Algeria, which was still in Africa. This was in 1953, one year before the start of the Algerian revolutionary armed struggle. He had already made contact with Algerian nationalists; so that when the revolution began, he was already integrated in the revolutionary movement. There is nothing surprising here. Many wonder why Fanon went to Algeria or what relationship could there have been between a man from Martinique and Algeria. The answer is simple: there exists a fundamental fraternity between all colonized people and between people colonized by the same foreign power. The Algerian revolution was not alien to Fanon.

In 1957, the French government expelled us from Algeria. We went to Tunisia, where the Front for National Liberation maintained its external branch and where they later created the Algerian Revolution's Provisional Government.

Fanon worked within the F.N.L and the Provisional Government. He was also interested in news dissemination. In 1960, they appointed him the Provisional Government's Ambassador to Accra.

We can retrace Fanon's itinerary. From his condition as an individual under French rule to his consciousness as a black man through his experience in a colonial society—up to a superior level and his adherence to the wider cause of the Algeria Revolution and still another level, the African Revolution in general.

Even before his ambassadorship to Accra, Fanon had taken part in a number of African people's conferences, including the first one held in 1958. During the conference, he made contacts with other African leaders of that period notably Patrice Lumumba, Felix Moumié of the Cameroon and President Kwame Nkrumah. The field of his experience and action widened and resulted in the writing of *The Wretched of the Earth*.

CF: Do you know what were Fanon's plans after the publication of *The Wretched of the Earth* ?

J.Fanon: It is always difficult to say what an individual like Fanon would have done if he had not died when he did. In his life, two things interchanged constantly. He would certainly have maintained his political activities. However, I cannot say with certainty where. No doubt, he would have stayed in Algeria—at least for a while. He had fought for its independence and because Algeria was a country very dear to him. This is, in fact, what I have done. The other important factor was his scientific interests. He was a psychiatrist and had never abandoned his research in that or other medical fields. He always practiced medicine even while involved in politics and writing.

CF: He was not what you would call a professional revolutionary then.

J.Fanon: That's right, he was not a professional revolutionary. He was a man very much opened to reality. In fact, everything he wrote he based on his personal experiences not on abstract theories.

CF: In the context of recent African history, how would you judge Fanon's work since his death?

J.Fanon: All that has happened in Africa since independence in 1960-62 demonstrates the accuracy of Fanon's points of view. Oppressed and colonized people cannot free themselves other than through armed struggle. That was the case of the Portuguese colonies and the case of what is now taking place in South Africa. How can there be a negotiated solution for majority rule there? The conflicts of the past few years in Zimbabwe, South Africa and Namibia demonstrate that fact. To pretend that blacks can achieve majority rule there through a negotiated solution is an illusion and a trick. Africans in that part of the continent will have to wage a very prolonged and protracted armed struggle. Moreover, I do not believe that they can succeed without the solidarity of the black American people.

CF: Going back to Fanon's birthplace—the French-speaking Antilles, what is the colonial situation there?

J.Fanon: When Fanon left Martinique, conditions there were not as clearly defined as they are today. He never stopped thinking of Martinique. I think he would be more concerned today, because underneath their departmental status, Martinique, Guadeloupe, and Guyane are just French colonies with another name. I believe that he would put all his energy in the service of his country (Martinique) and the Caribbean region in general.

CF: Can you say a few words about Fanon's relationship with the Negritude poets, Aimé Césaire and Léon Damas?

J.Fanon: Fanon had been Césaire's student in Martinique. For him, Césaire, Damas, and others like them were very important in his intellectual evolution as regard to the consciousness of his own negritude. He admired Césaire and Damas greatly. Nevertheless, he had already understood that, politically, Césaire could have done much more for the independence of Martinique. Independence is the sine qua non of political freedom. Even if neo-colonialism is active in a country, it is preferable to colonialism and total dependence. National liberation is a first step; without it, very little can be done. Without independence, nation building cannot begin.

CF: When *The Wretched of the Earth* was published, Jean Paul Sartre prefaced it. In subsequent editions, Sartre's preface is removed. Why?

J.Fanon: It was through my initiative that Sartre's preface to *The Wretched of the Earth* was removed. Let us say that from a western point of view, it is a good preface. Sartre understood the subject matter in *The Wretched of the Earth.*

But in June 1967, when Israel declared war on the Arab countries, there was a great pro-Zionist movement in favor of Israel among western (French) intellectuals. Sartre took part in this movement. He signed petitions favoring Israel. I felt that his pro-Zionist attitudes were incompatible with Fanon's work.

Whatever Sartre's contribution may have been in the past, the fact that he did not understand the Palestinian problem reversed his past political positions.

CF A great deal has been written about Fanon. If you have kept up with what has been written, what is your reaction?

J.Fanon: Indeed a number of Western intellectuals have written about Fanon. In my opinion, they have not completely understood his works. There is still much more to be written. I think, however, that it is in Africa and here in the US in the African American community that valid works about Fanon will be carried out.

CF: What do you think of the English translations of Fanon's works?

J.Fanon: I don't think—and knowledgeable people have told me—that *The Wretched of the Earth* is perfect; there are some lacunae and translation errors. In general, the English text does not reproduce the breadth, the dynamism, or the flow of the original French.

CF: Some critics say there is a fundamental contradiction between Fanon's works, what he stood for, and the fact that he married a white French woman. How do you answer these critics?

J.Fanon: It is my opinion, and I believe that it was also his—otherwise he would not have contracted nor remained in this interracial marriage—that there was no contradiction. In his works, he states clearly that it is through a revolutionary process that we can understand and resolve racial problems. Otherwise, we find ourselves in dead-end situations that are impossible to resolve—the sort that we can never put to rest. For example, critics can reproach a black American for marrying an Arab woman because her skin is lighter than his is and so on, and so on.

In a certain phase of the struggle, such a position can have for a time a positive and beneficially unifying effect. However, it remains a limitation. We are not going to limit each other to race! Otherwise, where is the revolution?

We can draw a parallel between such personal problems and the concept of Negritude, which Fanon analyzed. In his opinion—and this was later proved true—Negritude was but a stage in the dialectical process of the black man's struggle for liberation.

END

Notes

Preface

1. V.S. Naipaul, *The Middle Passage.*
2. Walter Rodney, *How Europe Underdeveloped Africa.*
3. Jack Moddis, *Introduction to Neo-Colonia l ism,* 62.

Introduction—Spain's Gambit

1. Eric Williams (ed), *Documents in West Indian History, Volume I*, 33.
2. Ibid., 144-145.
3. Eric Williams, *From Columbus to Castro*, 41–42.
4. Idem., *Documents,* 151.
5. As quoted in Lilyan Kesteloot, *Intellectual Origins of the African Revolution.* See also Benjamin Matip, *Heurts et Malheurs des Rapports Europe-Afrique Noire dans l'Histoire Moderne.*
6. Paul Edwards (ed.), *Bertrand Russell : Why I Am Not a Christian and Other Essay on Religion and Related Subjects*, 13.
7. Williams, *Documents,* 270.
8. Ibid., 218
9. Ibid.
10. Ibid., 207.
11. C.L.R. James, *The Black Jacobins*, 5.
12. Williams, *Documents*, 142.

Chapter One

1. Williams, *Documents*, 278.
2. Ibid., 279.
3. David Lowenthal, *West Indian Societies*, 42.
4. Williams, *The Negro in the Caribbean*, 4.
5. Lowenthal, *West Indian Societies*, 27.
6. Shelby T. McCloy, *The Negro in the French West Indies,* 10.
7. Williams, *From Columbus to Castro*, 145.
8. Lowenthal, *West Indian Societies*, 42.

Chapter Two

1. This was the sub-title of the Code Noir. The document under study dates from 1742, the oldest edition in existence.
2. Michel Leiris, *Contact de Civilisation en Martinique et en Guadeloupe*, 19.

3. Williams, *Columbus to Castro*, 188.

4. Acoma: *Revue de Littérature, de Science Humaines et Politiques Trimestrielle*, 51.

5. Racial groups: Blanc, griffe, mamelouc, marabout, métis, mulâtre, nègre, quarteron, sacatre, sang-mêlé.

Chapter Three

1. Julien Raymond, *Véritable Origines des Troubles de S. Domingue, et des Différentes Causes qui les Produits*, 3–4.

2. Prior to this date, a May 15, 1791, decree gave civil rights only to men of color whose parents had been free at the time of their birth.

3. Byan Edwards, An Historical Survey of the French Colony of the Island of St. Domingo, xix–xxi.

4. Ibid.

5. McCloy, *Negro in the French West Indies*, 75.

6. Ibid., 80.

7. As the men of color sought support from other blacks to defeat the whites, so did the French from the more numerous slaves to defeat the British and Spaniards to keep their colonies. E. Hayot, *Les Gens de Couleurs Libres du Port-Royal, 1629–1823*, 134.

8. McCloy, *Negro in the French West Indies.*

9. One often hears, particularly in Martinique, the hypothesis that Guadeloupe is less assimilated to France than Martinique or Guyane because "it is less mixed." See Frantz Fanon, *Pour la Revolution Africaine*, 21.

10. Cited in T. Adélaide, *Les Antilles Française,* 8.

11. Ibid.

12. Général Ménard au Ministre de la Marine, *Le Chef de l'Etat Major, Général de l'Armée au Ministre de la Guerre,* 1802 (Inventaire de la série colonies. C7A) Archive National.

13. Gabriel Manotaux et Alfred Martineau, eds., *Histoire des Colonies Française et de l'Expansion de la France dans le Monde,* 596.

Chapter Four

1. Raymond F. Betts, *Assimilation and Association in French Colonial Theory, 1890–1914*, 17.

2. André Siegfried, "La Psychologie du Français," in *La France Vue par les Français,* 65.

3. McCloy, *Negro in the French West Indies*, 24.

4. Jean-Paul Sartre, *Orphée Noir,* 22.

5. Gordon Martin, *Histoire de l'Esclavage dans les Colonies Françaises,* 11.

6. "Mémoire du Roi pour servir d'instruction au Sieur Conte Amiral Jacob" in J. Adélaide, *Les Antilles Française,* 11.

7. Ibid.

8. Herbert Ingram Priestly, *France Overseas, A Study of Modern Imperialism*, 66.

9. McCloy, *Negro in the French West Indies*, 134.

Chapter Five

1. Victor Schoelcher, *Abolition de l'Esclavage; Examen Critique du Prejugé Contre la Couleur des Africains et des Sang-Mêlés.*

2. Schoelcher, *Des Colonies Françaises; Abolition Immédiate de l'Esclavage*, xv.

3. Ibid., *Des Colonies Françaises,* xv-xvi.

4. In the latter part of the 19th century, France made Saint-Louis, Dakar, Gorée, and Rufisque French communes, and their populations French citizens.

5. Major among them were Protestant leaders and the Freemasons. See Gaston Martin , Histoire de l'Esclavage dans les Colonies Françaises, 285.

6. Schoelcher, *Abolition de l'Esclavage.*

7. Nombre probable de la population esclave esclave à l'époque de l'émancipation; déduction faite des enfants de 5 ans et andessous et des veillards de 60 ans et andessus. Archives Nationales, Colonies, K2.

8. Eric Williams, *Columbus to Castro*, 354.

9. Leaders of the Romantic School, such as Victor Hugo and Schoelcher, raised an army to defend the republic. They were defeated at the barricade of Faubourg Saint Antoine. Hugo, Schoelcher and others went into exile. Schoelcher was a Guadeloupe representative at the time.

10. See Acoma, Edition Maspero, Paris (janvier–mars, 1971) 48.

11. See Arvin Murch, *Black Frenchmen: The Political Integration of the French Antilles*, 20.

Chapter Six

1. Lettre du Gouverneur Général A. Vaillant au Ministre de la Marine, 9 Septembre 1851, Archive de la Martinique.

2. William L. Shirer, *The Collapse of the Third Republic,* 70.

3. Ibid.

4. See Brian Weinstein, *Eboué*, 16, 22; also Michel Leiris, *Contacts de Civilisation en Martinique et en Guadeloupe*, 81; McCloy, *Negro in the French West Indies*, 202; *Annuaire Statistique de la Guadeloupe, de la*

Martinique et de la Guyane, Institut National de la Statistique et des Etudes Economiques pour la Métropole et la France d'Outre-Mer.

5. Aguibou Y. Yansane, *Education in West Africa, First World: An International Journal of Black Thought,* (May-June 1977) 27, 62.

6. Ibid.

7. Brian Weinstein, *Eboué*, 184.

8. Jean-Paul Sartre, *Frantz Fanon, Fils de la Violence.* Supplément à *Les Damnés de la Terre.*

9. Raymond F. Betts, *French Colonial Theory*, 20.

10. Frantz Fanon, *Pour la Révolution Africaine*, 23.

11. René Belbenoit, *Dry Guillotine: Fifteen Years Among the Living Dead*, 57.

12. Ibid., 52.

13. Brian Weinstein, *Eboué*, 67.

Chapter Seven

1. Edith Kovats-Beaudoux, "A Dominant Minority: The White Creoles of Martinique," in Lambros Comitas and David Lowenthal (ed) *Slaves, Freemen, and Citizens: West Indian Perspectives*, 252.

5. 2. Charles Wagley and Marvin Harris, *Minorities in the World: Six Case Studies*, 103.

2. Kovats-Beaudoux, *Dominant Minority*, 252.

3. Albert Memmi, *Portrait du Colonisé Précédé du Portrait du Colonisateur*, 88.

4. Ibid., 48–49.

5. Ibid., 42.

6. Médéric-Louis-Elie Moreau de Saint-Méry, *Whites in a Slave Society* [editor's title] in Comitas and Lowenthal, *Slaves, Freemen, and Citizens*, 61.

7. Ibid., 53.

8. Ibid., 71.

9. Ibid., 68.

10. Ibid., 57–58.

11. Raphael Tardon, *La Caldeira*, 141–142.

12. Kovats-Beaudoux, *Dominant Minority*, 259.

13. Darcy Ribeiro, *The Americas and Civilization*, 304.

14. Ibid.

15. Kovats-Beaudoux, *Dominant Minority*, 263.

16. Julien Raymond, Homme de Couleur de Saint Domingue, *Observations sur l'Origine et les Progres du Préjugé des Colons Blancs contre les*

Hommes de Couleur, 9.

17. Julien Raymond, *Origines des Troubles de S. Domingue*, 4.
18. See Stendhal, *Le Rouge et le Noir.*
19. Julien Raymond, *Origines des Troubles de S. Domingue*, 4.
20. McCloy, *Negro in the French West Indies*, 29.
21. Ibid.
22. Julien Raymond, *Origines des Troubles de S. Domingue*, 3.
23. Ibid.
24. Ibid., 1.
25. Ibid., 5.
26. Eric Williams, *From Columbus to Castro*, 190.
27. Julien Raymond, *Origines des Troubles de S. Domingue*, 13.
28. McCloy, *Negro in the French West Indies,* 29.
29. Gabriel Debien, "Le Maronage aux Antilles Française au XVII Siecle," *Caribbean Studies*, vol. 6, no. 3.
30. Dean Hurault, "Histoire des Noirs Refugiés Boni de la Guyane Française," *Revue Française d'Histoire d'Outre Mer*, vol. 47, no. 166.
31. David Lowenthal, *West Indian Societies*, 187.
32. Leonard Sainville, *Dominique Negre Esclave*, 74.
33. Nellis Raynard Crouse, *French Pioneers in the West Indies: 1624–1664*, 101.
34. James G. Leyburn, *The Haitian People*, 19.
35. Louis-Xavier Eyma, *Les Peaux Noirs*, 127.
36. Eric Williams, *From Columbus to Castro*, 168.

Chapter Eight

1. H. P. Davis, *Black Democracy*, 36.
2. Julien Raymond, *Réflexion sur les Véritables Causes des Troubles et des Désastre de nos Colonies, Notamment sur ceux de Saint-Domingue*, p 19.
3. Ibid.
4. Ibid., 20.
5. Ibid.
6. Ibid., 27.
7. Ibid., 14.
8. Ibid., 36.
9. The constitution is reported in Louis-Joseph Janvier, *Les Constitutions d'Haiti*, 8–23.
10. Ibid., 3.
11. Ibid., 23.
12. Franklin D. Parker, "Political Development in the French Caribbean" in *The Caribbean: British, Dutch, French, United States* edited by

Curtis Wilgus, 99.

13. James G. Leyburn, *The Haitian People*, 4.

14. Janvier, *Les Constitutions d'Haiti*, 32.

15. McCloy, *The Negro in the French West Indies*, 112.

16. Ibid.

Chapter Nine

1. Lowenthal, *West Indian Societies*, 250.

2. C. A. Bissette, Lettre a Monsieur Agenor de Gaspin sur son discour pronouncé dans la séance du 4 Mai en faveur de l'abolition de l'esclavage, 1.

3. Ibid., 2.

4. Ibid., 3.

5. McCloy, *The Negro in the French West Indies*, 136.

6. The pamphlet was published in Paris in 1823 and signed "Avilla." The pseudonym was later traced to Bissette.

7. Melvin D. Kennedy, *The Bissette Affair and the French Colonial Question*, 56.

8. Mercer Cook, *Five French Negro Authors*, 47.

9. Alfred Martineau and L. Ph. May, *Trois Siecles d' Histoire Antillaise*, 231–2.

10. Ibid., 172.

11. J. Rennard, *Précis d'Histoire de la Martinique*, 101.

12. Emile Alcindor, *Les Antilles Françaises, Leurs Assimilation Politique a la Métropole*, 63.

13. Frantz Fanon, *Black Skin, White Mask,* 18.

14. Alcindor, *Les Antilles Françaises*, 98.

15. Brian Weinstein, *Eboué,* 8.

16. See André Malraux, *Anti-Mémoirs*, 112.

17. Frantz Fanon, *The Wretched of the Earth,* 54.

18. Ibid.

19. Aimé Césaire, *Cahier d'un Retour au Pays Natal*, 126–128.

20. André Haliar, *Dans les Départements d' Outre-Mer du Colbertisme au Gaullisme*, 115–116.

Chapter Ten

1. Bertrand Russell, *Why I Am not a Christian*, 128.

2. Jack Corzani, *Littérature Antillaise: Poésie*, 25.

3. Ibid., 26.

4. Jean Price-Mars, *De Saint Domingue a Haiti*, 15.

5. George Saintsbury, *A Short History of French Litérature*, 481.
6. George Pompidou, *Anthologie de la Poésie Française*, 32–33.
7. In Thomas Bennette, *La Pléiade Haitienne*, 5.
8. Ibid.
9. In Louis Moorhead, *Anthologie d'un Siecle de Poésie*, 45.
10. Auguste Viatte, *Histoire Littéraire de l'Amérique Française*, 398.
11. Ibid., 355.
12. Price-Mars, *De Saint Domingue a Haiti*, 18.
13. Ibid., 20–29
14. In Duraciné Vaval, *La Litérature Haitienne*, 197.
15. In Viatte, *Histoire Littéraire*, 392–393.
16. Ibid., 392.
17. Ibid.
18. Ibid., 396.
19. Ibid., 398.
20. Roger Faillard, *Etzer Vilaire Témoin de nos Malheurs.*
21. Etzer Vilaire, *Les Dix Hommes Noirs*, in ibid., 106.
22. Ibid., 107.
23. Ibid., 126.
24. Ibid., 113.
25. Ibid., 47.
26. Ibid., 115.
27. In Duracinés Vaval, *La Litérature Haitiennes*, 104.
28. Ibid., 103–106.
29. Ibid., 110.
30. Haitian writers often published their own works in volumes seldom totaling more than 300 copies. According to August Viatte there was in Port-au-Prince at the turn of the century one bookstore, no public library, and few private ones.
31. Antenor Firmin, *De l'Egalité des Races Humaines*, xiii.
32. In Michael Talley, *The Relationship Between Afro-Americans and Haitians*, 24–25.
33. Roger Gaillard, *Etzer Vilaire*, 46.
34. Victor Schoelcher, *Esclavage et Colonisation*, 197–198.
35. Ibid.
36. Ibid., 197.

Chapter Eleven

1. In Jack Corzani, Litérature Antillaise: Poésie, 86–7.
2. Victor Duquesnay, *Les Martiniquaises*, 6.

3. Corzani, *Littérature Antillaise*, 130.
4. Ibid., 142.
5. Ibid., 148.
6. Daniel Thaly, *Le Jardin des Tropiques*, 21.
7. Corzani, *Littérature Antillaise*, 130.
8. René Maran, *Le Livre du Souvenir*, 12.
9. Weinstein, *Eboué*, 21.
10. Ibid., 19.
11. Frantz Fanon, *Toward the African Révolution*, p. 19.
12. Weinstein, *Eboué*, 110–111.
13. None of these poets were professional writers. For the most part, they were men in liberal professions who wrote poetry as a hobby.
14. The term is used in G. Mosca et G. Bouthoul, *Histoire des Doctrines Politiques*, 262.
15. Interview with Léon G. Damas, February 7, 1977. Also see Lilyan Kesteloot, *Les Ecrivains Noirs de Langue Française: Naissance d'une Littérature*, 83–84. Also, see Weinstein, *Eboué*, 81.

Chapter Twelve

1. René Maran, *Batouala*, 75–78.
2. Ibid., 11–12.
3. Ibid., 12–13.
4. The depiction of the 1922 Jonathan Cape English translation of *Batouala* read in part: "When a novel of negro life, written by a full-blooded negro gains distinction of the Goncout Prize; when it appears with a label indicating that 8,000 copies are being sold daily; when it is made the subject of an interpellation in the Chamber and of heavy rebukes in the 'Temps' – then it may reasonably be assumed that the book is something out of the ordinary. And so it is."
5. Ibid., 12.
6. Ibid., 18.
7. In answer to a journalist's question as to why Jean-Paul Sartre was not jailed for his activities during the 1968 student rebellion, de Gaulle answered: "one does not imprison Voltaire."
8. Ibid., 13.
9. Interview with L. G. Damas, February 7, 1977.
10. Weinstein, *Eboué*, 81.
11. Oruno Lara, *Question de Couleur*, in Corzani, *Littérature Antillaise*, 221–222.
12. Ibid., 223.

13. *Batoula* was banned in the colonies, but West Indians in France mailed a great number of copies to family and friends at home.

14. Léon G. Damas, *Antologie des Poetes d' Expression Française*, p. 7.

Chapter Thirteen

1. Davis, *Black Democracy*, 279.
2. Thomas A. Bailey, *A Diplomatic History of the American People*, 554.
3. *The Crisis*, "Editorial," volume 10, September 1915, 232.
4. James Weldon Johnson, "The Truth about Haiti," *The Crisis*, volume 10, September 1920, 217.
5. Davis, *Black Democracy*, 273.
6. Ibid., 245.
7. Michael Talley, The Relationship between Afro-Americans and Haitians, 36.
8. Gustave Lebon, *Les Lois Psychologiques de l'Evolution des Peuples*, (1894) cited Haiti as proof of racial crossbreeding.
9. Robert Cornevin, *Jean Price-Mars (1876 – 1969)*, Preface to Jean Price-Mars, Ainsi Parla l'Oncle, 21.
10. Price-Mars, *La Vocation de l'Elite*, 1.
11. Idem, *La Vocation de l'Elite*, 15.
12. Ibid., 16.
13. Ibid., 176.
14. Ibid.
15. La Trouée, (n.p., June 1927).
16. Normil Sylvain, "Chronique-Programme," *La Revue Indigene*, Juillet 1927, 9.
17. Normil Sylvain, "La Jeune Littérature Haitienne," *La Revue Indigene*, Aout 1927, 53.
18. Ibid., 52.
19. Ibid.
20. Ibid.
21. Maurice Delafosse, *Les Noirs de l'Afrique*. See also Delafosse, *Civilisation Negro-Africaines*.
22. Leo Frobenius, *Histoire de la Civilisation Africaine*.
23. Jean Price-Mars, "Ainsi Parla l'Oncle ... La Famille," *La Revue Indigene*, Juillet 1927, 31.
24. Jean Price-Mars, *Ainsi Parla l'Oncle*, 44.
25. Ibid., 44–45.
26. Ibid.

27. Ibid.
28. Cornevin, *Jean Price-Mars*, 21.
29. Price-Mars, *Ainsi Parla l'Oncle*, 256.
30. Ibid.
31. Ibid., 257.
32. Ibid.
33. Ibid., 255.
34. Kleber George-Jacob, *Témoignage sur la Vie et l'Oeuvre du Dr. Jean Price-Mars*, 237.
35. Léon G. Damas, "Price-Mars: The Father of Haitianism," *Presence Africaine* (June–September 1960).
36. Davis, *Black Democracy*, 261.
37. Ibid.
38. Bernard Diederich et Al Burt, *Papa Doc et les Tontons Macoutes*, 45.
39. Léon Laleau, *Musique Negre*, 9.
40. Ibid., 21.
41. Léon Laleau, *La Releve*, Juillet 1933, 22.
42. Jean Price-Mars, Foreword to Jacques Roumain, *La Montagne Ensorcelée*, 9.
43. Jacques C. Antoine, "From Toussaint L'Ouverture to Jacques Roumain," in Mercer Cook, *Introduction to Haiti*, 119.
44. Jean Price-Mars, "A Propos de la Renaissance Negre aux Etats Unis," *La Releve*, Juillet-Aout-Septembre 1932.
45. Lorimer Denis, "Une Etape Littéraire," *La Tendance d'une Géneration*, 5.
46. Carl Brouard, "Doctrine de la Nouvelle Ecol *Les Griots* (Juillet-Septembre 1938) 2.
47. François Duvalier et Lorimer Denis, *Evolution Stadiale du Vodou.*
48. Jacque Roumain, "The Long Road to Guinea," *The Poetry of the Negro, 1746–1949*, 365-366.
49. Antoine, "From Toussaint L'Ouverture," p. 109.
50. Charles C. Pressoir, "La Mambo bans le Hounfort," *The Poets of Haiti*, 116.
51. Carl Brouard, "Le Tam-Tam Angoissé," *Les Griots* (Juillet – Septembre 1939), 18.
52. Claude Fabri, *L'Ame du Lambi*, 24.
53. In Ulrich Fleischmann, *Ecrivain et Société en Haiti*, 22.
54. Jean Brierre, "To Paul Robeson," *The Haitian American Anthology*, edited by Mercer Cook, p. 95.
55. Idem, "Me Revoici, Harlem," *Anthologie de la Nouvelle Poésie Negre et*

Malgache de Langue Française, edited by Leopold Sedar Senghor, p. 123.

56. Jean F. Brierre, "Me Revoici, Harlem," *Anthologie*, edited by L. S. Senghor.

57. Roumain, *Bois d'Ebene*, 5.

58. Roumain, "Nouveau Sermon Negre," *Anthologie*, edited by L. S. Senghor, 119–120.

59. Ibid.

60. René Dépestre, "Me Voici," *Etincelles*, 1–2.

61. Idem., "Je Connais un Mot," Ibid., 5.

62. Dépestre, "Le Baiser au Leader," Ibid., 18.

63. Emile Roumer, "The Peasant Declares his Love," *The Poetry of the Negro*, edited by Langston Hughes, 361.

Chapter Fourteen

1. Nathan Irvin Huggins, *Harlem Renaissance*, 55.

2. McCloy, *The Negro in France*, 212.

3. Huggins, *Harlem Renaissance*, 35; also *Men of Bronze* produced by WNET (New York: November 8, 1977).

4. Ibid., p. 57.

5. Shelby T. McCloy, *The Negro in France*, op. cit., p. 211.

6. Mercer Cook, "The Race Problem in Paris and the French West Indies," *Journal of Negro Education*, xi.

7. René Maran, *Le Livre de Souvenir*, 14.

8. Claude McKay, *If We Must Die*, 14

9. Langston Hughes, *The Big Sea*, 228.

10. Alain Locke, *The New Negro: An Interpretation*, ix.

11. Ibid., 6.

12. Ibid., 11.

13. Langston Hughes, *The Weary Blues*, n. p.

14. Langston Hughes, "The Negro Artist and the Racial Mountain," *The Nation*, 64.

15. W. E. B. DuBois, *The Soul of Black Folk*, 46.

16. Cited in Huggins, *Harlem Renaissance*, 179.

Chapter Fifteen

1. William L. Shirer, 20th Century Journey: "A Memoir of a Life and the Times," *Book Digest*, 151.

2. J. Ayodele Langley, *Pan-Africanism and Nationalism in West Africa, 1900 1945*, 287.

3. Ibid.

4. Ibid., 297.
5. La Redaction "Editorial" in *La Revue du Monde* Noir # 1.
6. Ibid.
7. Interview with Aimé Césaire, Fort de France, 31 July 1971.
8. Paulette Nardal, "Race," *La Revue du Monde Noir* # 6 *op. cit.*
9. Ibid.
10. "Editorial" in *Légitime Défense*, 1.
11. Ibid.
12. "Editorial," *Légitime Défense*, 1.
13. Ibid.
14. Ibid.
15. René Ménil, "Généralité sur l'écrivain de couleur antillais," *op. cit.*, 9.
16. Ibid.
17. Ibid.
18. Etienne Léro, "Misere d'une Poésie," ibid., 10.
19. Ibid.
20. Ibid.
21. Ibid.
22. L. G. Damas, *Poetes d'Expression Française*, 15.
23. David Thomson, Democracy in France Since 1870, 196.
24. William L. Shirer, *The Collapse of the Third Republic*, 233.

Chapter Sixteen

1. Interview with L.G. Damas, February 7, 1977.
2. Ibid.
3. Hughes, "The Negro and the Racial Mountain," *The Nation,* 64.
4. Interview with L. G. Damas, Washington, D.C., February 7, 1977.
5. Webster's New International Dictionary, 2nd ed., 1934. The term is dropped from subsequent editions. (Note that *Negritude* was a term commonly used in the 19th century. It is mentioned in Ken Burns's *Civil War*, for example, from texts of the period.)
6. The *Petit Robert* dictionary gives 1948 as the date *Negritude* was first used.
7. Aimé Césaire, *Return to My Native Land*, 84.
8. Ibid., 100.
9. Ibid., 120.
10. Ibid., 128.
11. Aimé Césaire, "Conscience Raciale et Revolution Sociale," *L'Etudiant Noir*, I, no. 3 (May-June 1935), 1, 2. All subsequent quotes of

Césaire are from this source unless otherwise noted.

12. "An Interview with Aimé Césaire," preceding Discourse on Colonialism, 69.

13. L. Sedar Senghor, "Racism? Non Mais Alliance Spirituelle," *L'Etudiant Noir*, I, no 3 (Mai-June 1935), 2, 3.

14. Césaire, *Return to my Native Land*, 113, 114.

15. Ibid., 69.

16. Césaire, "Rapport présenté au Congres du Parti Progressiste Martiniquais" in *Oeuvres Completes*, 487.

17. Frantz Fanon, *Black Skin, White Mask*, 203.

Chapter Seventeen

1. Several *Pigment* poems were first published in the periodical *Esprit* in September 1934 and in *L'Etudiant Noir* in June 1935.
2. Interview with L.G. Damas, February 7, 1977.
3. The French surrealist, Robert Desnos, wrote *Pigment*'s preface.
4. L.G. Damas, "S.O.S," *Pigment*, 48.
5. Idem., "Su rune Carte Postale," ibid., 52.
6. L. G. Damas, "Et Caetera," *Pigment*, 79–80.
7. Césaire's homage to Damas August 31, 1978.
8. L.G. Damas, *Retour de Guyane*, 52.
9. Ibid., 163.
10. Ibid., 174.
11. Ibid., 203.
12. Ibid., 168.
13. Prophetic in the sense that some of the changes *Retour de Guyane* advocated such as the closing of the penal colony took place fourteen years later.
14. The *Mine de Rien* poems are at Howard University's Moorland Spingarn Research Center in Washington, DC, and in the Léon Damas Collection at the Schomburg Center, Harlem, New York City.

Chapter Eighteen

1. Legend has it that, until his return from a stay in Haiti in 1944, Césaire spoke with a marked stutter. (Interview with L.G. Damas.) His oratorical skill—never in his native Creole language—helped his candidacy for political office in Martinique and made him a speaker of international repute. See James Baldwin, *Nobody Knows my Name*, 41.
2. Fanon, *Toward the African Revolution*, 21.

3. Césaire, *Return to My Native Land*, 41–43.
4. Georges Robert, *La France aux Antilles (1939–1943).*
5. A [West Indian] in particular an intellectual who is no longer on the level of irony discovers his Negritude. Thus, while in Europe irony protects against the existential anguish, in Martinique it protects against the awareness of Negritude. Fanon, *Toward the African Revolution,* 19.
6. Ibid., 21.
7. Ibid., 23.
8. Ibid., 24.
9. Césaire, "Toussaint L'Ouverture" in *Oeuvres Completes*, 244.
10. René Ménil, "Situation de la Poésie aux Antilles," *Tropiques,* XI, 133.
11. René Ménil, "Une doctrine réactionnaire: La Négritude," *Action Revue Théorique et Pratique du P.C. Martiniquais.*
12. Susan Frutkin, *Aimé Césaire: Black between Worlds*, 25.

Conclusion

1. Price Mars, *Lettre Ouverte au Dr. René Piquion*, 26-27.

2. In Michael Crowder, *Sénégal: A Study in French Assimilation Policy*, 51.

3. Alain Peyrefitte, *C'etait de Gaulle*, tome 1.

4. Crowder, *Idem.*

5. Pathé Diagne, *Léopold S. Senghor ou la Négritude Servante de la Francophonie au Festival Panafricain d'Alger* Trente ans après.

6. March 16, 1964, Fort de France city hall remarks – "States cannot be built on specs." "On ne bâtit pas des Etats sur des poussières." In response to Césaire's question regarding autonomy. Of note is that the remark came after de Gaulle, impressed with his reception on his arrival in Martinique, told the crowd, "my God, my God how French you are!" Many thought de Gaulle had said *foncés (black)* and not *français* (French).

7. France gives 25 to 50 per cent tax reduction to its citizens who buy property in the "ex"- colonies. See Loi Girardin in *Institut National de la Statistique et des Études Économiques.*

8. Remarks at the National Assembly February 1978.

9. Fanon, *Black Skin, White Mask*, 219.

10. Fanon, "Fondement Réciproque de la Culture Nationale et des Luttes de Libération," *Présence Africaine, Deuxieme Congres des Ecrivains et Artistes Noirs,* Tome I, 87.

11. Léro, "Misere d'une Poésie," 11.

Bibilography

A. Archives

Archives Nationales de France, Section d'Outre-Mer. Sous-serie C7A, C8A, C14. Paris: France.

"Annales des Antilles," Archives Départementales 1810 – 1848.

Archives du Ministere de la France d'Outre-Mer. Paris: France

Archives National de France. Fort de France: Martinique.

Archives National d'Haiti. Port-au-Prince: Haiti.

B. Anthropological, Historical and Sociological Works

Alcindor, Emile. *Les Antilles Françaises.* Paris: V. Girard et F. Briere, 1899.

Bellegarde, Dantes. *La Resistance Haitienne.* Montreal: Editions Beauchemin, 1937.

Corzani, Jack. *Histoire de la littérature des Antilles–Guyane.* Paris: Désormeaux, 1978.

Damas, L.G. *Retour de Guyane.* Paris: Librarie Jose Corti, 1938.

Delavignette, Robert. *Les Vrais Chefs de l'Empire.* Paris: Gallimard, 1939.

Diagne, Pathé. *Léopold S. Senghor ou la Négritude Servante de la Francophonie au Festival Panafricain D'Algier Trente ans après.* Paris: Editions L'Harmattan, 2006.

Edwards, Bryan. An Historical Survey of the French Colony in the Island of St. Domingo. London, 1797.

Eyma, L.-X. Les Peaux Noires. Paris: Michel Levy, 1857.

Fanon, Frantz. *Black Skin, White Mask.* New York: Grove Press, 1967.

———. *The Wretched of the Earth.* New York: Grove Press, 1968.

Labat, Jean-Baptiste. *Voyage du Pere Labat, aux Isles de l'Amerique.* 6 vols. The Hague: P. Husson, 1724.

Lasserre, Guy. *La Guadeloupe: Etude Geographique.* Bordeaux: Union Française d'Impression, 1961

Malouet, V. P. *Collection de Mémoires et Correspondances Officielles sur l'Administration des Colonies, et Notament sur la Guiane Française et Holondaise.* 5 vols. Paris, 1802.

Martin, Gordon. *Histoire de l'Esclavage dans les Colonies Françaises.* Paris: Presses Universitaires de France, 1948.

Moreau de Saint-Mery, Mederic-Louis-Elie. *Description Topographique, Physique, Civile Politique et Historique de la partie Française de l'Isle Saint-Domingue*_[1797]. 3 vols. Paris: Société de l'Histoire des Colonies Françaises et Libraire Larose, 1958.

Nardal, Paulette. "Eveil de la Conscience de Race." *La Revue du Monde Noir*_vol. II, no. 6, April 1932, pp. 25–31.

Peyrefitte, Alain, *C'etait de Gaulle, tome 1*. Editions le Fallois-Fayard, 1994

Price-Mars, Jean. *Ainsi Parla l'Oncle*. Port-au-Prince: Imprimerie Compiegne, 1928.

———. De Saint Domingue a Haiti. Paris: Presence Africaine, 1959.

———. *La Vocation de l'Elite*. Port-au-Prince: Imprimerie Emond Chenet, 1919.

Raymond, Julien. *Observations sur l'Origine et les Progres Colons Blancs contre les Hommes de Couleur*. Paris: Belin, 1971.

Sable, Victor. *La Transformation des Isles d'Amérique en Départements Français*. Paris: Editions Larose, 1955.

Jack Moddis, *Introduction to Neo-Colonialism* (New York: International Publishers, 1967) p. 62.

Shoelcher, Victor. *Abolition de l'Esclavage*. Paris: Pagnerie, 1840.

———. *Des Colonies Françaises*. Paris: Pagnerie, 1842.

———. *Esclavage et Colonisation*. Paris: Presses Universitaires de France, 1948.

Weinstein, Brian. *Eboué*. London: Oxford University Press, 1972.

Williams, Eric. *Documents in West Indian History. Vol. I*. Port-of-Spain: PNM Publishing Co., Ltd., 1963.

C. Literary Works (Partial)

Césaire, Aimé. *Return to My Native Land*. Paris: Présence Africaine, 1968.

Damas, L.G. *Pigment*. Paris: Présence Africaine, 1972.

Poetes d'Expression Françaises. Paris: Seuil, 1947.

Duquesnay. *Les Martiniquaises*. Paris: Fischbacher, 1903.

Laleau, Léon. *Musique Nègre*._Port-au-Prince: Imprimerie de l'Etat, 1931.

Lara, Oruno. *Question de Couleur*. Paris: Librarie Universelle, 1923.

Maran, René. *Batouala; A Negro Novel from the French*. London: Jonathan Cape, 1922.

Maran, René. *Le Livre du Souvenir*. Paris: Présence Africaine, 1958.

Roumain, Jacques. *Bois d'Ebene*. Port-au-Prince: Imprimerie Deschamps, 1945.

———. *Gouverneurs de la Rosee.* Port-au-Prince: Imprimerie de l'Etat, 1944.

———. *La Montagne Ensorcelee.* Collection Indigene. Port au-Prince: Imprimerie Chassaing, 1931.

Thaly, Daniel. *Le Jardin des Tropiques.* Paris: Editions du Beffroi, 1911.

Vilaire, Etzer. *Les Dix Hommes Noirs.* Port-au-Prince: Les Presses Nationales d'Haiti, 1972.

D. Manifestos (Primary)

Bernabé, Jean, Patrick Chamoiseau et Raphaël Confiant. *Eloge de la Créolité.* Paris: Gallimard, 1989.

Brouard, Carl. "Doctrine de la Nouvelle Ecole." *Les Griots* (juilet-septembre 1938), p. 2.

Césaire, Aimé. "Letter to Maurice Thorez." Paris: *Présence Africaine,* 1957.

Denis, Lorimer. "*Une* Etape Littéraire." *La Tendance d'une Generation,* (1934) p. 5.

Glissant, Edouard. *Le Discours antillais.* Paris: Seuil, 1981.

Hughes, Langston. "The Negro Artist and the Racial Mountain." *The Nation* (June 1926)

Léro, Etienne. "Misere d'une Poésie." *Légitime Défense* (June 1932) pp. 10-12.

Ménil, René. "Généralité sur l'Ecrivain de Couleur *Légitime Défense* (June 1932) pp. 7-9.

Sylvain, Normil. "Chronique-Programme." *La Revue Indigene* (juillet 1927) p. 9.

———. "La Jeune Litterature Haitienne." *La Revue Indigene* (Aout 1927) p. 53.

E. Anthologies

Collins, Marie (ed.) *Black Poets in French: A Collection of Caribbean and African Poets.* Totowa, N.J.: Scribner's, 972.

Eliet, Edouard (ed.) *Panorama de la Littérature Negro-Africaine (1921-1962).* Paris: Présence Africaine, 1965.

Haiti, Poetes Noires. Cahier special, no. 12, *Présence Africaine,* 1952.

Jones, Edward A. (ed.) *Voices of Négritude.* Valley Forge, Pa.: Judson Press, 1971.

Kennedy, Ellen Conroy (ed.) *The Négritude Poets.* N.Y.: Viking Press, 1974.

Kesteloot, Lilyan (ed.) *Anthologie Negro-Africaine: Panorama Critique des Prosateurs, Poetes et Dramaturges Noirs du XX Siecle*. Verviers: Gérard and Co., 1967.

Shapiro, Norman (ed.) *Négritude: Black Poetry from Africa and the Caribbean*. New York: October House, 1970.

Underwood, Edna Worthley (ed.) *The Poets of Haiti, 1782-1934*. Portland, Maine: Mosher Press, 1934.

F. Bibliographies

Baratte, Therese. *Bibliographie des Auteurs Africains et Malgaches de Langue Française*. 2d. ed. Paris: Cooperation Radiophonique, 1968.

Cameron, J. M. *Pan Africanism and Négritude: A Bibliography*, Ibadan, Nigeria: Institute of African Studies, University of Ibadan, 1964.

Jahn, Janheinz. *A Bibliography of Neo-African Literature from Africa, America and the Caribbean*. New York; Praeger, 1965.

Paricsy, Pal. "Selected International Bibliography of Négritude: 1960-1965." *Studies in Black Literature I*, (1970) pp. 103-115.

Zell, Hans and Helene Silvers (eds.) *A Reader's Guide to African Literature*. New York: Africana Publishing Corp., 1971.

G. General Works

Adelaide, T. *Les Antilles Françaises*. Paris: Desormeaux, 1972.

Bailey, Thomas A. *A Diplomatic History of the American People*. New York: Meredith Corporation, 1969.

Beaudoux-Kovats, Edith. "A Dominant Minority: The White Creoles of Martinique." *Slaves, Free Men, and Citizens: West Indian Perspectives*, edited by Lambros Comitas and David Lowenthal. New York: Anchor Books, 1973.

Belbenoit, René. *Dry Guillotine*. New York: E. P. Dutton, 1938.

Betts, Raymond F. *Assimilation and Association in French Colonial Theory, 1890-1914*. New York: Columbia University Press, 1960.

Crouse, Nellis M. *French Pioneers in the West Indies, 1624–1664*. New York: Columbia University Press, 1940.

Davis, H.P. *Black Democracy*. New York: Biblo and Thomas, 1967.

Debien, Gabriel. "Le Maronage aux Antilles Françaises" au XVII Siecle." *Caribbean Studies*, VI (October 1966).

Delafosse, Maurice. *Les Noirs de l'Afrique*. Paris: Payot, 1922.

Fleischmann, Ulrich. *Ecrivain et Societé en Haiti*. Quebec: Université de Montreal, 1976.

Freyre, Gilberto. *The Masters and the Slaves*. New York: Alfred A. Knopf, 1964.

Frobenius, Leo. *Histoire de la Civilisation Africaine*. Paris: Gallimard, 1925.

Frutkin, Susan. *Aimé Césaire: Black between Worlds*. Washington, D.C.: Monographs in International Affairs, 1973.

Guerin, Daniel. *Les Antilles Decolonisées*. Paris: Presence Africaine, 1956.

Haliar, André. *Dans les Départements d'Outre-Mer du Colbertisme au Gaullisme*. Paris: Editions Louis Soulanges, 1965.

Hanotaux, Gabriel and Martineau (eds.) *Histoire des Colonies Françaises et de l'Expansion de la France dans le Monde*. Paris: n.p., 1929.

Hatch, John. *A History of Postwar Africa*. New York: Praeger Publishers, 1970.

Houel, Orasta. *Cruauté et Tendresse*. Paris: Editions Payot, 1925.

James, C.L.R. *The Black Jacobins: Toussaint L'Ouverture and the San Domingo Revolution*. New York: Vintage Books, 1963.

Janvier, Joseph. *Les Constitutions d'Haiti*. Paris: C. Marpon et E. Flammarion, 1886.

Kennedy, Melvin D. "The Bissette Affair and the French Colonial Question." *The Journal of Negro History XLV* (January 1960) pp. 1–10.

Leiris, Michel. *Contact de Civilisation en Martinique et en Guadeloupe*. Paris: UNESCO, 1955.

Leyburn, James G. *The Haitian People*. New Haven, Conn.: Yale University Press, 1941.

Lowenthal, David. *West Indian Society*. London: Oxford University Press, 1972.

Malraux, Andre. *Anti-Memoirs*. New York: Holt, Rhinehart and Winston, 1968.

McCloy, S. *The Negro in France*. Lexington: University of Kentucky Press, 1961.

———. *The Negro in the French West Indies*. Lexington: University of Kentucky Press, 1966.

Memmi, Albert. *Portrait du Colonisé Précédé du Portrait du Colonisateur*. Utrecht: Presses Bosch, 1966.

Murch, Arvin. *Black Frenchmen: The Political Integration of the French Antilles*. Cambridge, Mass.: Schenkman Publishing Co., 1971.

Priestly, Herbert I. *France Overseas: A Study of Modern Imperialism*. New York: n.p., 1938.

Racine, Daniel. "Dialectique Culturelle et Politique en Guadeloupe et Martinique." *Presence Francophone XVII* (Automne, 1976) pp. 169–187.

Ribeiro, Darcy. *The Americas and Civilization*. New York: E.P. Dutton, 1972.

Russell, Bertrand. *Why I Am Not A Christian*. New York: Simon and Schuster, 1963.

Saint-Victor, D.B. *Haiti: Sa Lutte pour l'Emancipation*. Paris: n.p., n.d.

Sainville, Leonard. *Dominique, Nègre Esclave*. Paris: Fasquelle, 1951.

Salandre, H. and Cheyasse, R., *Histoire et Civilisation de Guadeloupe et Martinique: Les Antilles Françaises*. Paris: Ferrand Nathan, 1962.

Sartre, Jean-Paul. *Orphee Noir*. Paris: Presence Africaine, 1951.

Talley, Michael. "The Relationship between Afro-Americans and Haitians." Unpublished M.A. dissertation, Howard University. 1970.

Tardon, Raphael. *La Caldera*. Paris: Fasquelle, 1949.

Thompson, David. *Democracy in France since 1870*. London: Oxford University Press, 1969.

Vaval, Duracinée. *La Littérature Haitienne*. Paris: Bibliotheque Internationale d'Edition E. Sansotet Cie, 1911.

Viatte, Auguste. *Histoire Littéraire de l'Amerique Française* Paris: Presses Universitaires de France, 1954.

Wagley, Charles and Marvin Harris. *Minorities in the New World: Six Cases Studies*. New York: Columbia University Press, 1958.

Williams, Eric. *Capitalism and Slavery*. New York: Capricorn Books, 1966.

———. *From Columbus to Castro: The History of the Caribbean, 1492–1969*. New York: Harper and Row, 1970.

. *The Negro in the Caribbean*. New York: Negro Universities Press, 1969.

H. Evaluative Works

Aguessy, Honorat. "La Phase de la Négritude." *Presence Africaine* no. 80, (1971) pp. 33–49.

Antoine, Jacques. "From Toussaint L'Ouverture to Jacques Roumain," in *An Introduction to Haiti* edited by Mercer Cook. Washington, D.C.: Pan-American Union, 1951.

Bastide, Roger. "Variations on Négritude." *Presence Africaine* 8, no. 36 (1961) pp. 83–91.

Blair, Dorothy. "Whither Négritude?" *The Classic* (Johannesburg) 2, no. 2 (1966) pp. 5–10.

Cook, Mercer. "The Poetry of Leon Damas." *African Forum* 2, no. 4, pp. 129–132.

———. "Trends of Recent Haitian Literature." *Journal of Negro History* 32, April 1947, pp. 220–231.

Corzani, Jack. "Guadeloupe et Martinique: La Difficile Voie de la Négritude et de l'Antillanite." *Présence Africaine* no. 76, (1970) pp. 16–42.

La Difficile Presence

Damas, Léon G. "Price-Mars, the Father of Haitianism." *Présence Africaine* 4–5, nos. 32–33, (1960) pp. 204–218.

Dépestre, René. "Jean-Price Mars et le Mythe de l'Orphée Noir ou les Aventures de la Négritude." *L'Homme et la Société* 7 (1968) pp. 171–181.

Franklin, Albert. "La Négritude: Réalité ou Mystification? Réflexions sur 'Orphée Noir'" in *Les Etudiants Noir Parlent, Cahier Special Présence Africaine*, no. 14 (1953).

Gerard, Albert. "Historical Origins and Literary Destiny of Négritude." *Diogenes* no. 48, (1964) pp. 14–37.

Gleason, Judith Illsley. "An Introduction to the Poetry of Aimé Césaire." *Negro Digest* 19, no. 3, pp. 12–19.

Irele, Abiola. "Post-Colonial Négritude: The Political Plays of Aimé Césaire." *West Africa* 27 (Jan. 1968) p. 100– 101.

James-Sarreau, P. "Le Poerne de l'An Historique." *Présence Africaine* no. 74 (1970) pp. 210–216.

Towa, Marcien. "Aimé Césaire, Prophete de la Revolution des Peuples Noirs." *Abbia* no. 21 (1969) pp. 49–57.

——— . "'Les pur-sang' (Négritude Césairienne et Surrealisme)" *Abbia* no. 23, (1969) pp. 71–82.

Index

A

C

D

E

G

H

I

J

K

L

N

O

P

S

T

U

V

W

Z

About the Author

Dr. Christian Filostrat is a researcher in the field of French West Indies politics and literature and a life long student of the oral tradition and literature of Africa. He discussed the negritude struggle (agonistes) with Leopold S. Senghor, Aimé Césaire, and Léon Damas on several occasions. He was a friend of the Damas family while they resided in Washington, DC, and worked in Damas's library. (Mrs. Damas asked that he oversee the Howard University funeral service for her husband and ensure that his cremation followed her wishes.) He carried his ashes to Damas's final resting place in Guyane.

While in Dakar, President Senghor called him to discuss his article, "La Negritude et 'conscience raciale et revolution sociale' d'Aime Cesaire" and to ask that he lecture on the subject at the *Université des Mutants* on Gorée Island. In *Negritude Agonistes, Assimilation against Nationalism in the French-speaking Caribbean and Guyane* Filostrat presents *L'Etudiant Noir* where the negritude concept first saw light in 1935. Christian Filostrat is also the author of *The Beggars' Pursuit,* a novel that includes the negritude proponents' activities in Paris, circa 1936.

The Beggars' Pursuit

In his debut novel, Christian Filostrat deftly wove the lives of the Negritude proponents as students in Paris in the 1930s, resulting in a compelling political thriller that looks at the black elite in the French-speaking West Indies, Guyane, and Africa.

Fiction, political thriller
Pages, 336
Publisher, Africana Homestead Legacy Publishers
Hardcover with dust jacket
ISBN 978-0-9770904-5-7
Price $US 36
October 2007
Paperback
ISBN 978-0-9770904-7-1
Price $US 20
October 2007

A superb novel for sheer entertainment and study of African literature, culture, politics, and more. From Washington to the Democratic Republic of the Congo ...The saga of Ambassador Molu Sakeseba, Dictator Hector Motutu, Security Chief Maka Mgonu, Minister Fatou-Anne Cerusu, and U.S. State Department diplomats cleverly captures the interplay of Africa's elites with Western nations. Kudos to Filostrat for choosing a fascinating backdrop – the waning 20th century of conflicts and nascent democracies, dotted with colonial era flashbacks.

Edward Lama Wonkeryor, Ph.D.

African American Studies, Temple University, Philadelphia, Pennsylvania

CHRISTIAN FILOSTRAT
The Beggars' Pursuit

CPSIA information can be obtained at www.ICGtesting.com
Printed in the USA
BVOW072015131011

273524BV00004B/30/P

9 780981 89392